FROM IBM TO MGM

FROM IBM TO MGM

Cinema at the Dawn of the Digital Age

ANDREW UTTERSON

A BFI book published by Palgrave Macmillan

First published in 2011 by
PALGRAVE MACMILLAN

on behalf of the

BRITISH FILM INSTITUTE
21 Stephen Street, London W1T 1LN
www.bfi.org.uk

There's more to discover about film and television through the BFI. Our world-renowned archive, cinemas, festivals, films, publications and learning resources are here to inspire you.

Palgrave Macmillan in the UK is an imprint of Macmillan Publishers Limited, registered in England, company number 785998, of Houndmills, Basingstoke, Hampshire RG21 6XS. Palgrave Macmillan in the US is a division of St Martin's Press LLC, 175 Fifth Avenue, New York, NY 10010. Palgrave Macmillan is the global academic imprint of the above companies and has companies and representatives throughout the world. Palgrave® and Macmillan® are registered trademarks in the United States, the United Kingdom, Europe and other countries.

Cover design: Mark Swan
Cover images: (front) *Colossus: The Forbin Project* (Joseph Sargent, 1970), Universal Pictures; (back) *Alphaville* (Jean-Luc Godard, 1965), Chaumiane Productions/Filmstudio; *Westworld* (Michael Crichton, 1973), Metro-Goldwyn-Mayer
Designed by couch
Set by Cambrian Typesetters, Camberley, Surrey
Printed in China

This book is printed on paper suitable for recycling and made from fully managed and sustained forest sources. Logging, pulping and manufacturing processes are expected to conform to the environmental regulations of the country of origin.

British Library Cataloguing-in-Publication Data
A catalogue record for this book is available from the British Library
A catalog record for this book is available from the Library of Congress
10 9 8 7 6 5 4 3 2 1
20 19 18 17 16 15 14 13 12 11

ISBN 978–1–84457–323–3 (pbk)
ISBN 978–1–84457–324–0 (hbk)

Contents

Acknowledgments

Any book, though typically ascribed to a single author, is necessarily a collaborative act, one that depends on the contributions – obvious and less so – of a whole series of family, friends and colleagues.

In this instance, I am especially indebted to my PhD supervisors, Laura Mulvey and Charlie Gere, for their insight, guidance and encouragement while I pursued the doctoral research that informs this book. I am also grateful to my PhD examiners, Michele Pierson and Aylish Wood, who offered numerous helpful suggestions for shaping my ideas for publication.

I am thankful, too, to my employer, Canterbury Christ Church University, which has consistently supported my scholarly endeavours, via a research sabbatical, most significantly, as well as funding to attend and participate in international conferences. Meanwhile, engagement with colleagues and students has been vital in sustaining *joie de vivre* when faced with a computer and an empty page.

Alongside the more typical archival and other sources consulted in researching this book, a number of key 'protagonists' offered illuminating correspondence, the type of personal recollection and remembrance otherwise impossible to source. I am grateful in this respect to Ken Knowlton, Marvin Minsky, Michael Noll, John Whitney, Jr and Edward Zajac.

In terms of prior publications, if a number of chapters debuted, in one form or another, at various academic conferences and symposiums, Chapter 3 ('Tarzan vs IBM: Humans and Computers in *Alphaville*'), in particular, appeared in earlier shape in *Film Criticism* (vol. 33 no. 1, Fall 2008), and is revised and reprinted here by kind permission of editor Lloyd Michaels.

At Palgrave Macmillan (BFI Publishing), I am especially grateful to Rebecca Barden for her faith in this project and her expert guidance in steering it from conception to completion. As part of this process, the three anonymous readers who pored over my manuscript, offering diligent and detailed peer review, should be commended for the constructive and helpful nature of their comments.

Lastly, though a cliché, it is truly the case that this book would not have been possible without the unwavering support, enthusiasm and patience of nearest and dearest – parent, siblings, friends (a very special thank you, Jess Fulton).

Introduction

In the dawning digital age, following the flurry of technological and scientific research fuelled by the demands of World War II, the machines and expressions of cinema came together with those of the computer, as films and film-makers negotiated, articulated and projected an era increasingly rooted in digital devices. This cinema responded to the computer as a new technology, one with profound ramifications for the moving image and the wider world.

For the computer, to locate ourselves in history, this was a period of rapid proliferation. Following the development of the first commercially produced digital computers – in the wake of Remington Rand's UNIVAC (UNIVersal Automatic Computer), launched in 1951, building on earlier military machines designed in university laboratories – the computer was transformed, no longer a cloistered research tool restricted to the domain of specialist facilities. By the time equivalent machines intended for individual use – *personal* computers – were on the horizon, in the 1970s, the computer had become an established technology, occupying a central position in a world increasingly dependent on its usage.

Concomitant with this expansion, this period also gave rise to an equivalent growth in discourse concerning the computer. The visionary writings of Marshall McLuhan (see, for example, 1964, and with Quentin Fiore, 1967, 1968), Buckminster Fuller (including 1969a, 1969b, and, in direct reference to cinema, in the introduction to Youngblood, 1970) and others were not the first expressions of an early or proto-digital culture, for which one might look as near or far as Norbert Wiener's theories of 'cybernetics' (1948), Vannevar Bush's vision of a hypertextual Memex (1945), John von Neumann's conceptual mapping of computer architecture (1945), Alan Turing's proposed uses of a 'universal machine' (1936), Charles Babbage's design of an

Analytical Engine (1864), Augusta Ada King (Countess of Lovelace)'s principles of programming (1843) or to numerous other archetypes and antecedents that anticipated or accompanied the emergence of the machine later known as the 'modern', 'electronic' or 'digital' computer. Yet, the post-war period is unique in terms of an explosive proliferation, an intense expression of heightened hopes and amplified fears, the growing perception of impending revolution (for good or ill), and a time when the computer's fundamental forms, functions and meanings were malleable, still to be envisioned, proven and established in practice.

The burning question of what the computer could (or *should*) become (and whether, and in what forms, it would emerge as a tool for cinema) was explored by films and film-makers in myriad ways, on multiple levels. This period is replete with narratives steeped in digital themes and with attempts to adopt the computer as a creative tool. From subject matter to means of production, each aspect of this multifaceted engagement is central, not least in their intersections, to an understanding of what we refer to when we speak of cinema and computers, as one of the century's defining technologies found parallel expression in the moving image.

Cinema for Cybernated Life

In charting the technological and cultural processes by which cinema responded to the computer, this study ranges back and forth, between films *about* computers, on the one hand, and those produced *using* computers, on the other. By positioning these expressions as intertwined, to a certain extent synonymous, the intention is to elide the conceptual and methodological distance that has tended to separate them in historical and theoretical accounts. Notably, such an approach is consistent with changing conceptions of technology, more generally, where the technical and physical properties of tools, machines and devices are contextualised in intimate relation to the broader spheres of discourse in which they find meaning.

'Cybernated art is very important', wrote Nam June Paik in the particular context of art in the 1960s, 'but art for cybernated life is more important, and the latter need not be cybernated' (1966, p. 24). In defining the qualities that might constitute a distinctively digital art, Paik's assertion implies we must look beyond the physical means of production, which may or may not be extraordinary in terms of their own complexity, to also consider the capacity of art to engage with the wider world, itself infused with the computer's presence.

In applying Paik's model to film – though Paik himself was more concerned with television, video and other forms that lie beyond the purview of this particular study

– we arrive at a 'cinema for cybernated life', a grouping of films and film-makers whose collective legacy is the expression of the defining conditions of a period in which computers took on heightened meaning with regard to human experience. Inscribing this era's transformations, this cinema bore active witness to the computer's evolving position in the world, and would have been inconceivable without this backdrop.

While such engagement is defined by an exploration of the computer, its production was not always dependent on this technology. Beyond its own physical devices, an equally significant aspect of cinema's technological history – and how, in its relation to the computer, this history might be theorised – is the mediation and projection of technology. In responding to the computer, cinema occupied a more pivotal role than simply adopting the defining tools of the era. More ephemerally, but no less significantly, it also functioned as a site of cultural exchange, articulating but also negotiating the computer's social and symbolic status.

More generally, contemporary theories or models of technology are broad enough to encompass both concrete or tangible forms (objects, tools, artefacts and so on) and abstractions (including knowledge, discourses and determinants), with the former contextualised and understood in close relation to the latter.

In the context of science, as one example, Bruno Latour proposes the illuminating notion of 'technoscience' (1987) as a way of acknowledging the discourses that surround the established institutions and practices of scientific research. 'Technoscience', according to Latour, should account for more than just traditional laboratory science; it should include 'all the elements tied to the scientific contents no matter how dirty, unexpected or foreign they seem' (1987, p. 174). The essence of science, in other words, is just as usefully located in all that exists in relation to material manifestations.

To apply this model to cinema, mechanical underpinnings become the material, the tangible, the traditional. An examination of the connections between the moving image and the realms of discourse necessarily heightened in relation to the presence of technology – in this instance, the computer – invites an engagement with what has often been seen as 'dirty, unexpected or foreign', to return to Latour's phrase.

In considering the computer science of the dawning digital age, ideas encompassing a range of disciplines, practices and methodologies – from Claude Shannon's discussion of chess-playing computers (1950) and J. C. R. Licklider's concept of 'man–computer symbiosis' (1960) to Ivan Sutherland's system for computer-aided design (1963) and Joseph Weizenbaum's experiments in artificial intelligence (1966) – sought to identify the computer's potential uses and significance.

To a certain extent, films and film-makers contributed to the further generation of ideas, negotiating between the 'official' or 'legitimate' discourses of scientific research and the 'unofficial' or 'speculative' discourses of a flourishing technological imaginary. As an abstraction of computer science, the moving image formed part of a vanguard of cultural responses to scientific and technological developments only later fully absorbed or understood.

In responding to the computer's proliferation, cinema functioned as a conduit for the consciousness that arose in relation to this technology, inscribing the dreams and visions of our collective psyche, articulating and in turn shaping the attitudes towards the computer that circulated at this time. Technology, after all, might equally encompass the attitudes and anxieties – implicit and explicit – that propel our imaginings of machines, tools and physical devices.

For Wiebe Bijker, concerned with 'both the social shaping of technology and the technical shaping of society' (1995, p. 3), one cannot separate machines from the world in which they exist. 'One should never take the meaning of a technical artifact or technological system as residing in the technology itself', he suggests, outlining a concern with the factors that determine forms and functions. 'Instead, one must study how technologies are shaped and acquire their meanings in the heterogeneity of social interactions' (1995, p. 6).

The technologies of cinema – including the computer – are intimately bound up with this 'heterogeneity of social interactions', the competing discourses and determinants that permeate and infuse their application. Technology is more complex than the camera's multiple moving parts or the whirrs of the projector's mechanical breath, more ephemeral than the chips, circuit boards and other components of the computer. It is also recognised to include the multitude of resonances and reverberations that encompass the purely mechanical.

'Science and technology multiply around us', wrote J. G. Ballard in the introduction to his novel *Crash*. 'To an increasing extent they dictate the languages in which we speak and think. Either we use those languages, or we remain mute' (1975 [originally 1974], p. 47). In registering the computer's proliferation, as one instance of this multiplication, the cinema of the 1950s, 1960s and 1970s articulates such vocalisations. What film-makers shared was a willingness to bring cinema into direct contact with the computer, whether on the level of representation (with the computer typically pathologised as a fundamental threat to humanity, projected according to a series of hyperbolic anxieties, rendered as cinematic spectacle) or production (as film-makers grappled with the potential of what Gene Youngblood described as 'the aesthetic machine' [1970, pp. 189–93], exploring and exploiting the essential qualities of the new tools being embraced).

Whether in its adoption of the computer as a creative tool, or in imaginative reflections on this technology and its wider implications, this cinema articulated the changing conditions of increasingly digital times. Approaching these modes of discourse as intertwined – in dialectical dynamic, in this particular study, as we leap from chapter to chapter – goes some way to acknowledging the complex cultural conversation that was occurring at this time. In some instances, these strands or expressions are in harmony (anticipating, paralleling, interleaving), at other times in disharmony (juxtaposing, contrasting, contradicting). Yet, at all times, these different but related ways of coming to terms with the computer shed light on this technology's evolving status and its increasing presence in and via the moving image.

Cinema and the 'Universal Machine'

> It is possible to invent a single machine which can be used to compute any computable sequence.
>
> Turing, outlining his vision of a 'universal computing machine' (1936, p. 241)

In detailing the computer as a cinematic machine, the chapters that follow construct a historically located cartography of the ways in which cinema responded to the emergent computer. This technology was explored in experiments that spanned a range of cultural contexts, and which reveal both the competing discourses of a charged historical moment and the overarching contours of an extended process of technological change, as film-makers sought to incorporate the 'universal machine' into their diverse practices.

In proposing a newly charted history, or prehistory, this act of framing reveals, or brings into relief, a process of technological change – one that would continue, in one form or another, beyond the historical boundaries of this study – illustrating the ways in which the moving image responded to and in turn utilised the computer.

Accordingly, I have attempted to identify certain exemplars or major tendencies to illustrate this process, whose arc is outlined, but whose every detail has not been attempted. In broad terms, we move from symbolic impingement, in the 1950s (with the thematic exploration of anxieties concerning the computer) to a period of further representations and practical experiments (with attempts to explore the scientific and aesthetic potential of this technology as a production tool) and, only later, by the 1970s, to the absorption of the computer and these experimental practices, adapted or normalised according to classical narrative frameworks and representational models, by a major Hollywood studio.

The focus, here, is primarily on the *digital* computer, as opposed to analogue or mechanical parallels and precursors. If 'digital computer' is now virtually synonymous with 'computer', in terms of contemporary parlance and understanding, this was not always the case. In bygone centuries, for example, even certain humans were referred to as 'computers' when they performed tasks of numerical calculation. More recently, the nineteenth and twentieth centuries gave rise to countless pre-digital, mechanical devices designed to calculate, tabulate and otherwise process programmed instructions – in short, to compute.

If the transition to digital devices is a historical grey area (with significant overlap and an extended period where one might encounter both analogue and digital machines), and ostensibly technical or specialist in nature, the distinction between analogue and digital is nevertheless important to the seismic shifts of the era under consideration. Beyond a distinction between the continuous signals of analogue representation, on the one hand, and the discrete (or discontinuous) zeroes and ones of binary code, on the other, the power, flexibility and above all universality – to reprise Turing – of the digital computer, rooted in its distinctive code, led to a fundamentally evolved conception of what this technology might be and do.

The computer's anthropomorphised manifestation in *Forbidden Planet* (below) and *The Invisible Boy* (opposite)

As a starting point for cinema's mediation, Chapter 1 analyses Walter Lang's *Desk Set* (1957) – a film produced with the assistance of IBM, bridging 'fact' and 'fiction', with historical developments mobilised by characters and storylines – arguably the first film to foreground the digital computer as a primary subject. Moreover, beyond potentially reductive questions of teleology and origins, if Lang's film is more typically noted for its romantic pairing of Spencer Tracy and Katharine Hepburn (paralleling their off-screen relationship and reprising their on-screen roles), it is significant here as a revealing instance of the rich discourse that accompanied the computer's proliferation. While not necessarily alone in dealing with computers, *Desk Set* differs from its contemporaries – the fantastical visions of *Gog* (1954, Herbert Strock), *Forbidden Planet* (1956, Fred Wilcox) and *The Invisible Boy* (1957, Herman Hoffman), among others – in dissociating this technology from a primary concern with robots, and by engaging explicitly with the profound social significance of the 'electronic brain' – as early computers were popularly

known – a machine whose ultra-efficiency is represented, in this instance, as a threat to the jobs and livelihoods of those who work in the film's office setting.

Desk Set also differs from other films of the 1950s that depict computers – digital or otherwise – in that it is not an example of science fiction, nor does it represent an imagined future. While technophobia is typical of science fiction representations of outlandish sources of technological threat, *Desk Set*'s exploration of the computer's ideological and other implications occurs within the more humdrum environment of a typical workplace. In this scenario, as part of a fluid movement between specific technological developments and their narrative re-enactment, the computer becomes as significant a protagonist – or, more accurately, an antagonist – as any of its human counterparts, as *Desk Set* engages with a historical world in which the computer was finding symbolic meaning, but also physical presence.

In terms of such presence, if the computer was being marketed as a business machine, an efficient tool at the service of capitalist labour – as seen in, and represented by, *Desk Set* – it was not yet a technology conducive to the particular 'labour' of film-making – at least, in relation to those institutions and individuals most typically associated with the moving image. As Chapter 2 reveals, the earliest films to be produced using computers emerged not from Hollywood, for example, but in avant-garde experiments with recycled military equipment, in terms of mechanical or analogue machines, and in the science laboratories of commercial research and development (R&D), in terms of digital variants.

That these films were produced in contexts far beyond those traditionally associated with cinema says much about the computer's status at this time. If *Desk Set* reveals its role in an expanding commercial market, it was still a tool largely restricted in practice and expectation to a number of specialist fields, dominated by a white-coated elite of technicians and engineers. Typically excluded were those without the resources to rent or purchase a computer and those who lacked the technical skills necessary to program its workings. For film-makers, there were few, if any, opportunities for access, with the 'hobbyist' interventions of John and James Whitney – in the former's *Catalog* (1961), for example, designed to demonstrate the potential of the Whitneys' computers, built from spare parts acquired through military surplus following the end of World War II – the exception that proves the rule.

It was at the research facilities of Bell Telephone Laboratories (Bell Labs for short) – a more typical site at which to encounter the computer, if not the moving image – that scientists helped pioneer the digital computer as a tool for animation, following the Whitneys' analogue or mechanical antecedents. Experiments included Edward Zajac's *Simulation of a Two-Gyro, Gravity-Gradient Attitude Control System* (1963) – arguably the first computer animation produced anywhere using a digital computer – as well as Ken Knowlton's *A Computer Technique for the Production of Animated Movies* (1964) and Michael Noll's *Three-Dimensional Computer-Generated Movies* (1965). The intention, expressly scientific, was to find new ways of advancing knowledge, utilising the computer to generate and communicate scientific phenomena through graphics.

By contrast, juxtaposing modes of discourse, a much less optimistic view of science and scientists, in their relation to the computer, is illustrated in Chapter 3 by Jean-Luc Godard's *Alphaville* [*Alphaville, une étrange aventure de Lemmy Caution*] (1965), loosely contemporaneous with the experiments underway at Bell Labs. While scientists in the historical world were exploring the computer's potential functions – including the production of moving images as a means of generating, understanding and disseminating scientific data – *Alphaville* offered a fictional representation of this machine as a technological manifestation of systems of scientific and technical knowledge. Godard's computer enslaves rather than liberates humanity, underpinning and symbolically epitomising a future society structured according to an ideology of unabated scientific and technocratic rationalism.

In this sense, *Alphaville* extends to one possible conclusion the tensions displayed in *Desk Set* – played out, in Godard's variation, in a futuristic scenario in which the conflict between human and computer has been resolved in the latter's favour. Where *Desk Set* depicts an initial struggle, *Alphaville* portrays a dystopian projection of a world in which this struggle has been well and truly lost.

The irony, of course, one that implicitly reflects a broader ambiguity or conflicted position at this time, is that cinema has always been rooted in technology, necessarily predicated on machines – the camera and countless other tools typically involved in the production of a film such as *Alphaville*. In the 1950s and 1960s, Godard and others utilised existing technology for production, while appropriating the computer, on the level of story, as a source of symbolic threat, projected as a technological 'other'.

Conversely – again, weaving to and fro between modes of cinematic discourse, as well as back and forth between amplified extremes of technophilia and technophobia – it is precisely the qualities that Godard depicted as so alien to the computer that many of the first film-makers to utilise this machine sought to elicit, investigating its capacity to facilitate, and even originate, such expressions. There is a fundamental tension between the narrative conception of the computer and the various applications first perceived for it by avant-garde film-makers in relation to primarily abstract films. As Chapter 4 suggests, key experiments in this area include Stan VanDerBeek's pursuit of a visual poetry – in, among other films, a series of shorts he termed 'Poemfields' (1967–71) – constructed through pixellated moving images, and the abstract animations of John Whitney – working in the later 1960s with digital rather than analogue computers, in films such as *Permutations* (1968) and *Experiments in Motion Graphics* (1967–8) – and his distinctive vision of graphics in motion, intended to impact directly on the spectator's emotions.

Notably, VanDerBeek and Whitney found access to the latest computers only through corporate sponsorship and industrial patronage – through Bell Labs and IBM, respectively – in creative collaboration with designated technologists. These revised working relationships were typical of a broader coming together of artists and technologists (or, seen another way, the collapsing of the distinction between these respective roles), with artists of all kinds drawing on the applied research of computer scientists, engineers and technicians. The art and technology movement that flourished during this period – exemplified by Experiments in Art and Technology (EAT) – sought to explore the role of the traditional arts, including film, in the context of a changing technological environment.

Cultural initiatives such as Experiments in Art and Technology occurred alongside the further proliferation of films concerned with the computer on the level of representation, as this technology increasingly entered mass consciousness. Films such as Stanley Kubrick's *2001: A Space Odyssey* (1968), which deals with questions of artificial intelligence, resonated with a popular or collective imagination concerning computers and their role in society – as considered in Chapter 5. Irrespective of whether Kubrick's depiction has since transpired, or will ever transpire, it offers useful historical insight into a series of philosophical ideas concerning the computer's heuristic capabilities, at a time when more and more responsibility – in space travel and beyond – was being ceded to such machines.

Notably, it is again IBM that features prominently in charting cinema's relation to the computer. In *2001: A Space Odyssey*'s thinly veiled reference to IBM – albeit consistently denied by the film-makers, including co-screenwriter Arthur C. Clarke (see 1972, for example, where he refers to the supposed allusion as an 'annoying and persistent myth', p. 78) – in the form of the spaceship's onboard computer HAL (an acronym that resembles the name of the global computer corporation when each letter is advanced by one digit), we witness a revealing example of how the computer's existence in the historical world became inseparably intertwined with its projection through cultural form. IBM occupied a material and mythological presence: on and off screen in *Desk Set*; referenced in *Alphaville* and Godard's working title, 'Tarzan vs IBM'; as a corporate sponsor of film-makers and their experiments with computers; and so on. Beyond a more familiar existence at the forefront of the burgeoning computer industry, IBM also functioned as a potent cultural signifier, already an important element of this era's cultural mythology.

The cosmic expansion explored by *2001: A Space Odyssey*, not least in the psychedelia of its celebrated 'Stargate Corridor' sequence – filmed using a variation of the 'slit-scan' technique pioneered by John Whitney, a further intertwining, or even 'intertwingling' (1974, p. DM45), to borrow Ted Nelson's term – found parallel expression in the late 1960s and early 1970s in the phenomenon of 'expanded cinema' (see Youngblood, 1970), as charted in Chapter 6, with Whitney's films, and the computer, again at the fore.

Against the potent backdrop of a countercultural current of radical techno-Utopianism, 'expanded cinema' sought to match expanded consciousness with a multimedia conception of art, with film – and its technologies – situated alongside the revelatory potential and combinatory possibilities of other forms, old and new. For avant-garde film-makers, the computer formed part of an updated set of tools, alongside the related electronic forms of television, video, oscilloscopes, holography and other variations.

To conclude, ending where more typical histories tend to begin, Chapter 7 details a symbolic moment of institutional adoption or absorption, the recontextualisation of this experimentation within Hollywood, as the commercial film industry arrived at a means of utilising the computer as a narratively integrated special effect – nearly two decades after *Desk Set*. In Michael Crichton's *Westworld* (1973), computer graphics – programmed by John Whitney's son, John, Jr, connecting the commercial film industry and avant-garde – convey the visualisation of an android's point of view, with pixellated imagery a corollary of the decidedly digital subjectivity of the film's fictional foe. Though this footage accounts for only a few minutes of the final cut, it nevertheless represents a symbolic integration into the popular cultural landscape, with the experiments of previous years adapted for an altered institutional setting, in industrial terms, and collapsed within classical narrative orderings, in stylistic terms.

In some respects, we come full circle, with the fictional scenario depicted in *Desk Set* – the negotiation between a series of industrial systems and an existing technological apparatus, on the one hand, and the possibilities associated with the computer as a new technology, on the other – beginning to occur within the commercial film industry. Where the mathematical underpinnings and information storage capacities of the computer rendered it suited to the office setting of Lang's film, in the 1950s, it was not until this technology had evolved as a machine capable of producing graphics that might be incorporated within a classical narrative, that a major studio – Metro-Goldwyn-Mayer (MGM), in the instance of *Westworld* – sought to integrate this technology.

Affirming the universality conceptualised by Turing, the 'universal machine' had become one of the key technologies of the post-war era, and by the 1970s a part of the technological expressions of Hollywood. Reflecting rapid proliferation, the computer had come to serve a range of needs within society, not least its potential uses by film-makers, across a range of different contexts, who sought to pioneer and establish Turing's theoretical model as an applicable tool.

Excavating the Past, Projecting the Future

> In the past century it has come to be generally acknowledged that, in the words of Wyndham Lewis, 'The artist is always engaged in writing a detailed history of the future because he is the only person aware of the nature of the present.'
>
> McLuhan, exploring the 'extensions of man' (1964, p. 65)

Acutely aware of this 'present', and responding to, and at times perpetuating, the type of scenario that Alvin Toffler popularly described as 'future shock' (1970), referring to the ruptures and repercussions that accompany accelerated technological change, the films and film-makers explored in these chapters collectively articulate the highly charged period that saw the computer's mass proliferation. In terms of historiography, the aim is to frame and extrapolate the continuing revelations of this 'detailed history of the future', establishing links between occurrences that may not initially appear to be related, with the moving image employed as a lens that allows us to excavate the past and reveal visions of the future.

In doing so, the positing of a purview and the construction of connections are necessarily conscious acts, with methodological implications. For instance, wary of imposing retrospective logic at the expense of recognising and preserving inherent complexity, Thomas Elsaesser warns of the potential dangers of 'retroactive causalities' (2004, pp. 85–92), challenging the neat trajectories and absence of loose ends that characterise most accounts of film history – concerned with technology or otherwise – constructed according to 'the modes of temporal sequence and causal disposition by which historians make sense of the continuities and ruptures, the lines of force and the piles of fragments in the records of human actions and events' (2004, p. 104). Elsaesser's contention is that complex, discrete and discontinuous occurrences are typically distorted in historical orderings as connected and continuous, simplified according to an overwhelming and irresistible causality.

Siegfried Zielinski, for his part, affirms that 'The history of the media is not the product of a predictable and necessary advance from primitive to complex apparatus' (2006 [originally 2002], p. 7). Yet, media histories typically understand the process of technological change – in terms of cinema, from sound and colour to 3-D, widescreen and beyond – as one of absorption and restabilisation, demonstrating how emerging technologies are integrated into existing institutions and established practices. The problem, Zielinski suggests, is that such historiography is overly concerned with, and therefore determined by, 'hegemonial relations and conditions' (1999 [originally 1989], p. 9), with an exclusive emphasis on what Elsaesser refers to as the 'winners' (2006, p. 22) of history, defined in teleological terms from an *a posteriori* perspective – relative rather than absolute.

While not conforming to every tenet or detail of the methodological antidotes proposed by Elsaesser and Zielinski – each of whom offers compelling variations on the idea of 'media archaeology', suggesting adventurous unearthings (see Elsaesser, 2004, 2006; Elsaesser and Hoffmann, 1998; Zielinski, 1999, 2006) – this study seeks to offer an 'archaeology'-inspired historiography, challenging a simple, one-dimensional trajectory of technological change as occurring according to inevitable, linear, causal momentum, and a shift from primitive tools to complex technology that finds relevance and meaning only in commercial application and exploitation.

For example, reprising the notion of technology as conceptualised in terms of a multiplicity of discourses and determinants, the computer's evolution and its connections with the moving image are historicised across diverse contexts (including Hollywood, but also extending far beyond) and modes of discourse: from feature films to avant-garde experiments and scientific shorts, with ideas generated, circulated and communicated through moving images, primarily, but also in related scientific papers, magazine articles, trade journals and other sources (augmented by more recently conducted author interviews, further reflecting on this period via memory and recollection).

In charting this multiplicity, the intention is to complicate one-dimensional conceptions of technology, first, and traditional historiographic trajectories of commercial mastery – as defined solely from the perspective of the dominant industry, i.e. Hollywood – second, by considering the kaleidoscope of heterogeneous voices and expressions, a plurality of perspectives, often competing, that encompass a range of cultural contexts. To reprise Elsaesser, where 'retrospective causalities' are constructed, it is to explore rather than efface complexity.

Nor, to return to Zielinski's critique of 'hegemonial relations and conditions' as the overriding impulse for much of media history, is this study's purview defined exclusively in terms of commercial integration as a prelude to a *necessary* and *inevitable* sense of linear, continuous 'progress' towards the tools and expressions of today. If our conclusion is reached with an example of Hollywood's utilisation of the computer as a production tool, this is not to foreground this instance of technological absorption above all else, or to celebrate this process without question. Commercial exploitation is framed not simply as a 'year zero' to more recent or familiar history, but as a counterpoint to a prior period that pointed to, and continues to point to, multiple possible futures.

After all, what of the continuing revelations of an extended moment of *in*stability and *non*-standardisation, of genuine *un*certainty and *un*predictability concerning the role and impact of computers? And what of the discursive negotiations – spanning heightened extremes of technophilia and technophobia – that resulted from such rupture? Many of the most radical ideas concerning computers, more generally, and in relation to the moving image, in particular, were proposed during this earlier period. This study seeks to chart these ideas and expressions in all their hyperbole and hysteria, eccentricity and excess, tapping into the heightened discourse of a pivotal period.

Cinema operates, in the words of Claudia Springer, as 'a clean slate, or a blank screen, onto which we can project our fascination and fears' (1991, p. 322). As such, films articulate – and therefore reveal – something of the society that gives rise to them. Looking back, in terms of the computer, individual films become useful texts by which to uncover historically specific perceptions. The moving image preserves a layer of archaeological sediment, crystallising underlying preoccupations. The textual remnants left behind exist as a barometer of sorts, a gauge by which to extrapolate the future visions projected in cinema's past. By analysing such expressions, we can chart shifts in a cinema that reflects – or *refracts* – its historical moment.

Collectively, outlining the major developments that preceded cinema's widespread use of the computer, the films and film-makers explored in this study offer insight into the technological, cultural and historical contexts for the arrival of the digital technology – not least, the computer – now so central to society. They offer ways of making sense of a past period of profound technological change and a means of illuminating the present. Far from being blind to the now, the process of exploring and illuminating a turning point in history – an extended fracture in the predictable and a moment of shift that offers parallels and precursors to contemporary transformations – reveals the 'new' in the 'old', bringing us into revised relationships with contemporary digital culture and the state of cinema today.

Conclusion

The multifarious ways in which the moving image responded to the computer reflected, and played a part in, the shifting status of this technology, anticipating a time when it would come to occupy a position at the very centre of society, throughout much of the world. The computer's adoption by film-makers – from avant-garde cinema to the narratives of Hollywood – can be seen as a microcosm for a changing era, as this machine was ushered into the symbolic order and as its uses proliferated. If this technology was initially perceived as having only limited functions, in an even smaller number of fields – despite Turing's prescient postulation of universality – it evolved into a machine with applications in a wide range of contexts, not least in the realm of cinema.

As one of the means by which the computer's rise was mediated, cinema played an important role in establishing the significance and signification of this technology, offering a series of vivid visions and imaginative projections. Via intertwined strands of discourse, the computer is seen in multiple guises: as a productive device in the office, in *Desk Set*; as a means of scientific visualisation, in the computer animations of commercial R&D; as a dehumanising tool of technocratic control, in *Alphaville*; as an aid to creative collaboration, in the films of the art and technology movement; as an intelligent machine, a potential next step in our evolution, in *2001: A Space Odyssey*; as a route to new aesthetics and higher consciousness, in 'expanded cinema'; and as a tool for Hollywood special effects, in *Westworld*.

In seeking to make sense of the computer, film-makers grappled with a series of fundamental questions – What are its defining characteristics? Is it a machine to be embraced or feared? What are its implications and ramifications? – concerning its status in the context of cinema and the wider world. In hindsight, the answers to these and other questions have become clearer, if far from exhausted. Yet, as we shall see, it is at the dawn of the digital age that many of these questions were first raised and many of the most radical responses proposed.

[1]

Computers in the Workplace: IBM and the 'Electronic Brain' of *Desk Set* (1957)

In parallel with experiments in how to utilise the digital computer as a tool for the production of moving images, cinema played an important role in determining the evolving status and symbolic signification of this nascent technology, anticipating and in turn shaping its practical applications. Before the pioneering work of John and James Whitney, using analogue computers, would find digital equivalents, this machine was already being represented on screen, including in Walter Lang's *Desk Set*, adapted from the play by Walter Merchant (first performed in New York between 24 October 1955 and 5 July 1956).

In the 1950s, a time when the digital computer's forms and functions were still far from certain, concerted efforts were made by companies such as IBM to develop new applications and markets for this technology, involving a range of strategies that extended to the moving image. To establish a commercial presence in the wider workplace would solve twin productivity puzzles: first, how to sell digital computers in contexts beyond the military and other government sectors, from the perspective of the expanding computer industry; and, second, how the digital computer might serve to increase workplace efficiency, in terms of this industry's potential business clients.

The office workplace – the subject of *Desk Set*, a romantic comedy produced with the assistance of IBM – was one of the settings in which this ideological war was waged. If attempts by IBM and others to market the digital computer in this context were broadly welcomed by employers, they also represented a source of considerable anxiety for many employees. Such initiatives met with a range of negative responses: from fear and antipathy, in the majority of cases, to defiance and obstruction, more radically, as manifestations of a long tradition of resistance against mechanised or automated labour. At stake, it was believed, were the livelihoods of those who perceived their jobs, and very humanity, to be under threat, as part of an onslaught of advanced, automated technology, which might eventually supersede the human worker.

In representing this dynamic – a clash between the quest for the introduction of the digital computer into the workplace and the struggle to preserve the jobs of those who felt most immediately threatened by this technology – *Desk Set* played an active role in the very conflict it depicted. Resonating with the ideas of Vannevar Bush, J. C. R. Licklider and others, it projected an explicit vision of how the computer – or 'electronic brain' – should be received, at least according to IBM. In what ways did *Desk Set* negotiate prevailing attitudes concerning this technology's role in the workplace? Why utilise the romantic comedy, in particular, a genre not typically associated with technological themes? And for what reasons did IBM, a company with little or no obvious connection with the moving image, seek to participate so prominently in the production of Lang's film?

Digital Computers in the Office

Desk Set depicts the day-to-day happenings of a busy workplace, the research library of a fictional broadcasting company. Mirroring the dynamic of many real offices of the time, a number of giant computers are purchased. The film's intrigue – and, ultimately, its ideological core – rests on the central enigma of precisely whether these machines are intended to assist or replace the human worker.

Revealingly, the film opens with a wide-angle shot of a computer, emblazoned with the IBM corporate logo. The camera zooms in towards the machine that will dominate the ensuing narrative. As if to signify this importance, the opening credits emerge as printed output, including a statement – 'We gratefully acknowledge the co-operation and assistance of the International Business Machines Corporation' – that announces the role of IBM – 'a starring role' (Anon., 1957a, p. 12), according to the company's employee newsletter, *Business Machines*.

Desk Set was seen by IBM as an opportunity to promote the digital computer in an office setting – as opposed to military and scientific markets, most obviously – assuaging anxieties concerning the increasing prevalence of such machines in the workplace. The moving image would function as an ideological vanguard, preparing the public to receive and accept this relatively new technology, shifting popular perceptions from the technophobic to the technophilic. *Business Machines* highlighted this public relations effort, noting not only the prominent display of IBM equipment in the film, but also the involvement of one of the company's employees in training Neva Patterson for the role of computer operator Miss Warriner, with an emphasis on 'how to do a professional job before the cameras' (Anon., 1957a, p. 12).

For the producers of *Desk Set*, through Twentieth Century-Fox, the close relationship with IBM secured access to this expertise and the computers on which the film's fictional counterparts were based. According to Kevin Maney, biographer of IBM founder Thomas Watson, Sr, it was Wallace Eckert's SSEC (Selective Sequence Electronic Calculator) that provided much of the inspiration for the machine seen in *Desk Set* (2003, p. 355). This computer, according to Charles Bashe, was one of the most flexible and powerful of its time, 'the first machine to combine electronic computation with a stored program, and the first machine capable of operating on its own instructions as data' (1982, p. 296).

While historians such as Bashe still debate whether the SSEC was the first stored-program computer, Eckert's machine was also notable, in terms of its design and marketing, for Watson's decision to locate a unit within the ground-floor lobby of IBM's Madison Avenue headquarters, New York. An SSEC remained there between 1948 and 1952, when this model was replaced by the newer IBM 701. 'The lobby was open to the public', Maney explained, 'and its large external windows allowed a view of the SSEC for the multitudes cramming the sidewalks on Madison and 57th Street' (2003, p. 354). IBM's intention was to keep the SSEC running so that it could be viewed by anyone who looked in from the street. This exposure would serve both to increase public awareness and shape popular perceptions.

IBM's employee newsletter, meanwhile, identified the IBM 407 accounting machine as the source of the computer seen in *Desk Set*, after IBM's first choice – the IBM 705 data-processing system, a mainframe in the same series as the IBM 701, which replaced the SSEC – was ruled out by Twentieth Century-Fox, who 'wanted more movement' (Anon., 1957a, p. 12). The IBM 407, introduced in 1949, was one of the best known of IBM's accounting machines, or tabulators, and would typically be combined with associated devices such as a card punch.

Either way, a detailed model, which might best be thought of as resembling a number of IBM's computers, spanning digital as well as earlier, analogue machines, was created for use on set. Like the showcase SSEC, which comprised approximately 21,000 electromechanical relays and 12,000 vacuum tubes, the external architecture of the computer depicted in *Desk Set* is decorated with an array of dials, gauges, flashing lights and switches. As one reviewer noted, 'its exterior console houses some 9,000 light bulbs, ten miles of electrical wire and several dozen switches, faders, dimmers, flashers and special transformers' (Tozzi, 1957, p. 280). The computer was projected as a special effect – 'a wedding of mechanical perfection with dramatic effect' (Anon., 1957a, p. 12), as *Business Machines* put it – extending the process of signification already set in motion by the executives of IBM and their plans for the SSEC as public spectacle.

The external architecture of such machines, both in the historical world – where Watson is said to have told IBM designers to ensure that 'the SSEC looked sleek and impressive' (Maney, 2003, p. 354) – and in fictions such as *Desk Set*, functioned as important signifiers. As Patricia Warrick has argued:

> The process of handling information at incredible speeds within the computer cannot be visualized. All that actually can be observed are metal cabinets, keyboards, visual screens, rows of blinking lights. The electrons that convey information within the computer's circuitry cannot be seen, and the speed of the process, measured in nanoseconds, can hardly be comprehended.
>
> (1980, p. 6)

In the absence of methods for representing the nuances of internal operation, perceptions are formed through this proxy signification.

By the mid-1950s, and the production of *Desk Set*, IBM was already one of the key players in the nascent digital computer industry (see Bashe *et al.*, 1985; Pugh, 1995). The company's first foray into the digital computer market came in 1952 with the announcement of the IBM 701, a commercial scientific machine more popularly referred to as the 'Defense Calculator', after its perceived military market. This launch expanded IBM's focus from an existing dominance in the manufacture of standard punched-card machines.

The decision to actively pursue the production of digital computers followed the success of Remington Rand's UNIVAC (UNIVersal Automatic Computer). The first of these machines was received by the US Census Bureau in 1951, for the purpose of tabulating data, a transaction that effectively began the era of commercial digital computing. Notably, according to Paul Ceruzzi, the UNIVAC was a general 'information processing system, not a calculator' (2003, p. 30), and therefore had the potential to replace not only existing calculating machines, but also the people who operated them.

In terms of sales, the UNIVAC was ultimately overtaken by the IBM 650, developed after the IBM 701 and adopted by a wider commercial market. Introduced in 1954, this smaller unit was designed, like the IBM 701, for specialist scientific calculations, but it proved to be more versatile. This broad appeal encouraged IBM to diversify its production and marketing of the digital computer beyond its core clientele, towards the broader business market in which IBM had an established reputation for supplying office machines.

As these and other models became available, and as speed and memory increased and prices decreased, the digital computer took on an entrenched position in many business operations. Newly developed machines were introduced to replace activities that had previously involved less sophisticated tools, such as typewriters and filing cabinets. With its particular dependence on data processing, the office was thought to be an ideal setting for the introduction of digital computers, one that might make significant gains from automation. Commercial users turned to this machine in an effort to cut costs and reduce the number of employees involved in tasks they no longer needed to perform.

In *Desk Set*, such interests are represented most explicitly by Mr Azae (Nicholas Joy), president of the Federal Broadcasting Network, in whose offices the film is set. It is Azae, for instance, who authorises the purchase of the computer that causes such consternation within the reference department, headed by Bunny Watson (Katharine Hepburn). For Azae, the computer is perceived as a corporate panacea, reducing costs and increasing productivity.

There is a clear disparity between the company president's knowledge of the computer and the trust he invests in this machine. While mystified by the nuances of how a computer might actually work, in technical terms, he is beguiled by the potential benefits it might bring to the workplace. At one point, Richard Sumner (Spencer Tracy), who holds a PhD from the Massachusetts Institute of Technology (MIT) and has been hired to install the machine he invented, attempts to explain its workings: 'Visual read-offs are all centralized, miniaturized, and set on schematic patterns now ... and then the data compiled is all automatically computed ... and there's an automatic typewritten Panalog ...'. He is interrupted by Azae: 'Now, now, please wait a minute. I don't understand one word you're saying. [...] If you say it can be done, that's good enough for me.' The company president is willing to place his faith in the progress of technology, so long as it is at the service of increased productivity.

In this regard, the interests of management contrasted sharply with the concerns of those who worked at lower levels within such companies, and who feared rather than celebrated the introduction of computers. Newspaper headlines such as '"Brain" Is Hired' (Anon., 1956), 'Big Business Done in Big Computers' (Zipser, 1957), '"Brain" Seen Used in Office Routine' (Anon., 1952) and 'Electronic "Brain" Open for Business' (Anon., 1954) suggest the extent of the impingement of the 'electronic brain', as computers were popularly known in the 1950s, on popular consciousness.

Sceptical workers would need much more persuading from companies such as IBM if they were to be convinced that computers were not a threat to their existence.

In *Desk Set*, even the idea of this machine is enough to create widespread panic among the office workers. Watson is initially courted by IBM, which maintains a complex dual existence: closely linked to the production of the film, in the historical world, and referred to within the diegesis, in terms of its fictional scenario. She enters the reference department following a demonstration by IBM of an 'electronic brain', which is used to translate Russian into Chinese. Her reaction expresses the type of anxiety that soon reverberates around the entire office, as she describes the IBM computer as 'frightening', with the demonstration giving 'the feeling that maybe, just maybe, people were a little bit outmoded'.

The response of Sumner is to tease Watson, extending her thinking to its logical conclusion. 'Wouldn't surprise me a bit if they stopped making them', he remarks of the human worker. This comment, either deadly serious or a deadpan joke, points to the potential obsolescence of the likes of Watson, lampooning her relative inefficiency when compared with the machines produced by IBM and others.

Sumner refers to himself as a 'methods engineer', a role that involves the use of scientific applications to improve the relationship between productivity in the workplace and the number of hours expended by workers. The process of evaluation that Sumner undertakes at Azae's request mirrors what many businesses faced at this time. Companies would typically conduct feasibility studies before purchasing a computer, with such methods engineers searching for areas of labour that might be automated. In combining this analysis of systems with the introduction of a computer, Sumner is situated somewhere between the 'scientific management' (1911) of Frederick Taylor and the 'cybernetics' (1948) of Norbert Wiener.

The anxiety expressed by Watson, and fuelled by Sumner's insensitivity, quickly spreads throughout the office, when news breaks of the impending arrival of a computer similar to the machine demonstrated by IBM. Peg Costello (Joan Blondell), another office employee, yells of Sumner, 'He's trying to replace us all with a mechanical brain!', before jumping to the cataclysmic conclusion, 'That means the end of us all!' By contrast, Watson is more composed, and her response expresses a belief, not shared by her employers, in the superiority of the human worker. 'Calm down', she reassures Costello. 'No machine can do our job.'

The initial harmony or equilibrium within the reference department is ruptured, with the overriding concern that human workers will be outmoded by the computer's arrival, resulting in job losses. 'What do you suppose it'll be like here next Christmas when we are gone?', asks one employee, referring to the machine's impending arrival, 'I understand thousands of people are being replaced by these electronic brains.' Costello adds, 'If we do get canned, we won't be the only ones to lose our jobs because of a machine.' There is an explicit recognition of the broader social and technological backdrop against which the film's narrative is being played out.

The precedent of the payroll department, in particular, is raised by Costello as one instance where the fight to protect human workers, in the face of increasing automation, has been lost. After all, Sumner has already introduced a computer into the payroll department, resulting in the dismissal of half of its employees. Similarly, in the historical world, computers were likewise ensconced in the workplace as calculators or record-keepers, albeit restricted to relatively simple numerical applications, such as those involved in basic accountancy.

As early as 1832, Charles Babbage, who would later design his own influential computer (for a description of the Analytical Engine, see 1864, pp. 112–41), pointed to the potential capacity of machines to perform mental as well as physical labour. His discussion of 'economic machinery and manufactures' (1832) is framed in terms of the 'division of labour', a simplification of work tasks that would eventually lead to automation. 'The division of labour', he explained, 'can be applied with equal success to mental as to mechanical operations, [...] it ensures in both the same economy of time' (1832, p. 191). For Babbage, in other words, there is no necessary distinction between the application of machines to physical and mental labour.

Despite this postulation, the widespread application of the 'electronic brain' to mental tasks did not occur until much later, synchronised with the introduction of the digital computer into the workplace. The processing power and flexibility of this machine, as it existed in the 1950s, made it capable of driving an increasingly wide range of tasks. Its first applications, noted Harry Braverman, were 'large-scale routine and repetitive operations which to some extent were already performed mechanically: payrolls, billing, accounts payable and accounts receivable, mortgage accounting, inventory control, actuarial and dividend calculations, etc.' (1974, p. 328). Increasingly, however, the computer was also applied to new tasks, including 'elaborate sales reports, production-cost accounting, market research information, sales commissions, and so forth, all the way up to general accounting' (1974, p. 328).

In terms of complexity, the work involved in Watson's reference department is sufficiently differentiated from the 'routine and repetitive operations' described by Braverman for the office workers to make a stand, seeking representation from their union. That Watson, Costello and their colleagues feel so strongly about the computer's impending arrival reveals a delineation between their attitudes towards the adoption of computers in the payroll department, where the replacement of human workers is seen as inevitable, and its proposed introduction into the reference department, where mobilised resistance remains a viable option.

Human Workers and 'Electronic Brains'

In *Desk Set*, the computer's potential to perform mental tasks is pitted against that of its human counterparts, with the broader relationship between humans and machines constructed as an underlying symbolic opposition. The reference department setting, in particular, with its dependence on a range of mental operations, offers an ideal context for such exploration. The relative capabilities of the human worker and 'electronic brain' are compared and contrasted, juxtaposing the intellectual dexterity of the former with the processing power of the latter. If the computer can carry out the numerical operations of payroll, can it also complete the various research tasks undertaken within the reference department?

The 'electronic brain' introduced into the fictional scenario of *Desk Set* is Sumner's EMMERAC (Electro-Magnetic MEmory and Research Arithmetical Calculator) – the name of which references the fad for elaborate acronyms in naming the computers of the era – a machine that can store the contents of an entire library (for a discussion of *Desk Set*'s representation of the computer as an information storage and retrieval machine, see Malone, 2002). The complete text of William Shakespeare's *Hamlet*, as one example, is coded as decks of punched cards. The computer also takes on tasks previously performed by the department's human workers. In contrast to Watson and her colleagues, the EMMERAC is able to process complex calculations accurately and at incredible speed. It has total recall of data, meaning that access to information is almost instantaneous, and that information can be stored indefinitely. The EMMERAC also works tirelessly around the clock, with no capacity for boredom, performing data-processing tasks that human workers would perceive as mental drudgery.

The particular claim of Sumner, in relation to *Desk Set*'s office setting, is that the computer will increase productivity. At one point, he calculates that the EMMERAC will save 6,240 man-hours per year. Once all of the reference department's paper holdings have been fed into the computer, he demonstrates the machine's capacity. A complex computational task that would take a human operator three weeks to accomplish – 'How much damage is done annually to American forests by the spruce bud-worm?' (the answer to which is revealed as $138,464,359.12) – is performed by the EMMERAC in barely a minute, surpassing the ability of Watson and her colleagues to perform what amounts to a typical research task.

The office space of *Desk Set* with and without the EMMERAC

Such workings contrast sharply with those of the busy office setting into which the EMMERAC is introduced. Unlike the storage methods of the computer, for instance, the reference department is still very definitely paper-based, replete with the residue of physical data processing. Piles of documents and rows of filing cabinets are scattered throughout the office, with such detritus forming a key component of the film's *mise en scène*.

Watson's department grapples with the type of information overload anticipated by Vannevar Bush, in the historical world, when he proposed his Memex (a conflation of 'MEMory' and 'EXtender') (1945) – a machine that was never built, though its principles and proposed operations can be seen in many aspects of modern computing. Writing of the physical storage and access of information, he explained:

> There may be millions of fine thoughts, and the account of the experience on which they are based, all encased within stone walls of acceptable architectural form; but if the scholar can get at only one a week by diligent search, his syntheses are not likely to keep up with the current scene.
>
> (1945, p. 105)

Of particular concern for Bush was the area of scientific research, whose focus on information is not unlike the workings of Watson's reference department.

In relative terms, when compared with the computer, Watson and her colleagues perform tasks slowly and at times inaccurately. Even when Watson lies about how long it takes her department to perform the spruce bud-worm enquiry, in an attempt to compete with their technological adversary, the time she quotes is still eclipsed by the speed of the machine. In comparison with the EMMERAC, the office workers are also prone to memory lapses and unreliable recall, as well as 'flaws' such as tiredness and boredom when faced with repetitious tasks.

Beyond this initial comparison, however, the relationship between the human brain and 'electronic brain' is shown to be more complex than a straightforward or binary opposition. Their respective characteristics, in the context of the reference department, are shown to be more nuanced. A number of ambiguities are represented that challenge the fixed definition of human and computer as diametrically opposed.

Evidencing a degree of anthropomorphism, for instance, the EMMERAC is often referred to by the reference department workers in distinctly human terms. Specifically, it takes on a gendered identity, with the name 'EMMERAC' transformed at various stages into 'Miss Emily Emmy', 'Miss Emmy', 'Emmy', 'she' and even 'good girl'. In relation to the predominantly female office workers, the computer is delineated as being a gender-specific threat. While this technological 'other' is introduced by Azae and Sumner, male figures who represent power and authority, into a space otherwise dominated by women, the EMMERAC is projected not in the image of its male progenitors but in that of the female workers it is designed to replace. The message, for Carol Colatrella, is that women lose jobs to computers that are represented as female and not to their male colleagues, with *Desk Set* depicting the 'feminized machine, and not the male efficiency expert, as the enemy' (2001, p. 7).

Watson, in particular, is positioned as a romantic rival to the gendered computer, with each of these 'women' competing for the affections of Sumner. Indeed *Desk Set* was also known as *His Other Woman*, a title that foregrounds the love triangle formed between the two leads and the computer that comes between them. Playing with the conventions of the romantic comedy, the intimate relationship that Sumner shares with his machine is parodied as romantic union, with the EMMERAC a second love interest beyond Sumner's more conventional relationship with Watson.

The more generalised references to an 'electronic brain' are also an important part of the film's interrogation of the relationship between humans and computers. This biological metaphor, by which computers were popularly referred to in the 1950s – alongside references to 'mechanical brains', 'giant brains', 'electric brains' and the shorthand 'brains' – implies an equivalence between the workings of the human brain and the computer, with the latter approximating the neurological workings of the former.

The Memex represented one facet of a strand of thinking that proposed further parallels between the human brain and 'electronic brain' as a way of envisaging the operations of an intelligent computer. Bush proposed an intimate exchange between the two as a solution to the problem of working with vast amounts of information. Transcending the sheer computational power of the EMMERAC, the Memex was designed to replicate and extend the workings of the human brain, storing information according to the associational nature of memory. The mind, Bush explained, 'operates by association. With one item in its grasp, it snaps instantly to the next that is suggested by the association of thoughts, in accordance with some intricate web of trails carried by the cells of the brain' (1945, p. 106). The Memex was seen not as a literal equivalent of the brain's biological architecture, as many scientists proposed, but as a mechanical means of mirroring the broader principles of its workings.

While Bush saw the human mind as a model for computer logic, human involvement is also shown in *Desk Set* to limit the performance of certain operations. In terms of data input, for instance, the EMMERAC is as fallible as its human operators. Azae, indulging in some wishful thinking, describes the EMMERAC as a 'modern miracle', which will never make a mistake. Sumner corrects him, clarifying that the computer is only as reliable as the information it is programmed with. 'Emmy can make a mistake', he advises, 'but only if the human element makes the mistake first.' The computer will perform its calculations accurately, but only so long as it is programmed correctly, in the first instance, by its human operators.

Similarly, even in this reconfigured technological landscape, there are some areas of operation that are performed more effectively by Watson and her colleagues. Away from the EMMERAC, though the reference department is seemingly ramshackle and drowning in paper, the office workers nevertheless possess systems for negotiating this chaos. They improvise, often working from memory, without the mechanically augmented features of a machine such as the Memex. The human workers also possess a degree of personal charm and spontaneous interaction when dealing with the requests of clients. The impersonal EMMERAC, by contrast, with its primitive user interface and difficult operation, is unable to replicate this innately human quality.

More complexly, the dividing line between the respective capabilities of the human worker and 'electronic brain' is ultimately drawn at the capacity to evaluate and contextualise information. It is in these functions, above all, that the human workers excel, exercising judgments based on intuition and cultural knowledge. Even

Sumner, the inventor and patent holder of the EMMERAC, concedes that 'No machine can evaluate' when it is asked to do more than process programmed instructions.

When faced with culturally specific and polysemic meanings, in particular, the computer is unable to contextualise the data it processes. Much of the film's comedy is dependent on the polysemic nature of language, and the misunderstandings that arise out of this fluidity. A request for information on 'Corfu', for instance, 'The island [...] off the coast of Albania near the mouth of the Adriatic', is initially confused with 'curfew', 'A bell rung every evening. [...] Introduced into England by William the Conqueror.' Lived experience of the historical world is shown to be an important part of thinking, with human language quite unlike that of the EMMERAC. When Watson asserts that no computer can do her job, she is at least partly correct.

In terms of the message from management, the computer is sold to the reference department workers on the promise that it will liberate rather than replace them. The introduction of computers will make their jobs easier, simplifying through automation the complexities involved in research. 'The purpose of this machine [...]', suggests Sumner, describing the EMMERAC, 'is to free the worker [...] from routine and repetitive tasks and liberate his time for more important work.' The 'electronic brain' would be applied to tasks that involved the processing of large amounts of data or which required great speed and accuracy. The human worker, meanwhile, would engage in loftier pursuits, freed to become more 'human'. Work would be more varied, with menial or mundane activities replaced by opportunities to engage in more professional tasks.

Sumner's attempts to address the anxieties of those within the reference department who fear for their jobs are remarkably consistent with the rhetoric that emerged from IBM at this time, in the historical world. The company message, noted Emerson Pugh, an employee with IBM for several decades, was that computers 'were not designed to replace people. Rather they were designed to help people, by relieving them of drudgery' (1995, p. 143). As one instance of this expression, IBM CEO Thomas Watson, Jr declared that 'Machines might give us more time to think but will never do our thinking for us' (Anon., 1957b, p. 4), even going so far as to affirm that 'A machine, unlike man, is not original' (Anon., 1957b, p. 4).

Yet, what none of the characters in *Desk Set*, nor IBM in the historical world, reveal is the ultimate extension of such strategies of automation. For every potential benefit, the human worker might also face a heavy price, with technology deployed to deskill and ultimately replace the existing workers. Where Watson, Jr argued that 'It is essential for each of us to strive to retain originality and to maintain our identity

Office researchers and company management physically and symbolically divided

as human beings' (Anon., 1957b, p. 4), the workers of *Desk Set* fear this message to be precisely the opposite of what Azae has in mind with the EMMERAC. As such, a fundamental disjuncture exists between the interests of employers and employees, which is both revealed and exacerbated by the computer's arrival, and is, in an early scene of conflict, reinforced by *mise en scène* and framing that position these parties at extremes of the frame, literally and symbolically divided by the computer.

When the 'electronic brain' in the payroll department malfunctions, issuing notices of dismissal instead of pay cheques, this process appears to have been initiated. The individual and collective acts of resistance that are organised by the workers appear to have been to no avail. Though it ultimately transpires that the dismissal notices dispatched by the computer have been served in error, this pivotal moment – as close to a Freudian slip as a machine is capable – is nevertheless revealing, laying bare the conflicting attitudes of employers and employees towards the benefits or otherwise associated with the computer. The EMMERAC illuminates the blunt reality of one possible conclusion to the policy of automation undertaken by Azae. His company appears oblivious to the needs of its human workers and the outcomes associated with its introduction of the computer. Morale diminishes, leading to a profound sense of dislocation, with Watson and her colleagues increasingly disenfranchised.

Peace between Human and Computer

Of course, such a finale would do little for the public image of IBM – without whom the film may not have been made – and would have resulted in one of the least successful romantic comedies ever. After all, the theme of mass redundancy is neither romantic nor comedic. As such, the threat of rebellion in *Desk Set* is ultimately collapsed into a technologically mediated reconciliation of employers and employees. As the film moves towards its conclusion, there is a realisation that a new equilibrium can be achieved. Crucially, this resolution is arrived at without resorting to extremes: either the replacement of the human workers by the EMMERAC, on the one hand, or their further resistance to this technology, on the other.

An important part of achieving this harmony is the retention of the option, and its ultimate implementation, to 'pull the plug' on the EMMERAC. In actual fact, the same result is achieved by activating a red key that the workers are repeatedly warned not to touch. This safety mechanism is explicitly signified by its conspicuous colour and prominent placement. It is a last resort, deployed to override the machine if and when it malfunctions. The idea that the human workers retain the ability to turn off the EMMERAC is represented as being an ideal upon which the notion of acceptable technological progress is predicated.

In moving towards rapprochement, the relationship between the human workers and the EMMERAC is one that undergoes a significant process of transformation. For Watson and her colleagues, there is an eventual understanding that the computer, when properly applied, can actually enhance the work of the research team. While the value of the human brain is demonstrated, so too is the EMMERAC's potential to assist it.

For Azae, meanwhile, there is a recognition that the computer might complement rather than replace the company's existing workforce. There are limits, in other words, to the use of machines, such as the EMMERAC, to restructure work according to more efficient models of productivity. The desire to eliminate the human element in the reference department must be tempered, stopping short of the 'final solution' proposed by the malfunctioning computer in the payroll department. Indeed it is only when resolution is reached between the human workers and the computer that productivity gains can follow.

A research enquiry that epitomises this harmony is revealed when the reference department is asked: 'What is the total weight of the Earth?' No amount of defensiveness can prevent Watson and her colleagues from admitting that the laborious calculations involved in computing such a task could be performed more swiftly by the EMMERAC. Yet, it is also the case that the evaluative skills of the human workers are demonstrated as superior to the calculating abilities of the computer. Such qualities are necessary, in this instance, to determine whether the weight requested of the reference department is 'With or without people?'

In revealing the mutually beneficial relationship between humans and computers, *Desk Set* anticipated, in the context of labour, what Licklider would later describe as 'man–computer symbiosis' (1960). Following an exercise conducted in 1957 to examine his own use of machines, Licklider wrote of a coming together, the 'living together in intimate association, or even close union, of two dissimilar organisms' (1960, p. 4). The 'living together' that Licklider proposed would occur between mechanically extended man, on the one hand, and the artificial intelligence of the computer, on the other.

While Licklider acknowledged that computers were not yet capable of fully facilitating this symbiosis, his ultimate intention was 'to enable men and computers to cooperate in making decisions and controlling complex situations' (1960, p. 4). Like the fig tree pollinated only by a single type of insect, the *Blastophaga grossorum*, which in turn relies on the syconium of the fig tree for food and hibernation, humans and computers, though ostensibly dissimilar, likewise have the potential to coexist as collaborators. 'In the anticipated symbiotic partnership', Licklider continued, 'men will set the goals, formulate the hypotheses, determine the criteria, and perform the evaluations' (1960, p. 4). Computers, meanwhile, 'will do the routinizable work that must be done to prepare the way for insights and decisions in technical and scientific thinking' (1960, p. 4).

While the precise nature and degree of coexistence and collaboration envisaged by Licklider transcends the division of labour established in the reference department of *Desk Set*, the idea of symbiosis is nevertheless implemented as a broader philosophy. It is a means of selling the computer to sceptical workers, in the first instance, and of maintaining harmony in the office, beyond the initial introduction of this technology. The human worker and computer are represented as equivalent to the fig tree and insect conceptualised by Licklider, with each able to benefit from the other.

In this instance, the proposition is collapsed into the structure and generic parameters of the romantic comedy, with the hostility shown towards the computer contained according to the more benign narrative trajectory of heterosexual romance. Conventional romantic closure between Watson and Sumner – mirroring the off-screen relationship between Hepburn and Tracy, as well as their on-screen pairing in countless other films – is mediated through the EMMERAC, a machine that Watson must compete with for Sumner's attentions. The struggle to integrate the computer with the needs of the people it is shown to assist is mapped onto the contours and formulae of a genre that necessitates the romantic union of this initially antagonistic couple.

When Watson challenges Sumner to prove his love for her by allowing the machine he invented to malfunction, it is Watson who provides the hairpin – a device replete with gender connotations – that is used to repair the EMMERAC. If Watson's heart is to be won, Sumner's interest in the computer must be reconciled with an equal concern for the human operators who must now work alongside this machine. By the same logic, the computer's introduction into the workplace must balance the concerns of employers and employees if it is to achieve a full and productive symbiosis.

Conflict and resolution via the conventions of the romantic comedy

Conclusion

In depicting the relationship between Sumner and Watson as technologically mediated, *Desk Set* combines the conventions of the romantic comedy with a historically located commentary on the computer's role in the workplace. As a cultural representation, Lang's film deals with transformations in the historical world, revealing the ambiguities of being human at a time when equivalents of the EMMERAC were altering the social status of the human worker.

On the one hand, *Desk Set* expresses widely held anxieties concerning the computer, articulating these concerns and the material conditions that gave rise to them.

In looking back, it provides evidence of popular perceptions of this machine and its possible consequences. The reference department, a site of technological and ideological conflict, exists as a symbolic microcosm, representative of the computer's role in the working world of the 1950s.

On the other, as well as communicating certain attitudes, *Desk Set* played an important role in depicting the ideologically determined resolution of these concerns, as one constituent of a broader effort by IBM to smooth the computer's transition into new markets and a revised place in the social order. As a deliberate rhetorical strategy, it foregrounds anxieties concerning the threat posed by the computer in order to debunk them. The idea of opposition to this machine is not simply disregarded, nor is it countered by an entirely positive representation of IBM, Sumner or the EMMERAC. Rather, such anxieties are satirised, collapsed into the conventions of the romantic comedy and ultimately neutralised through the resolution of the mythical opposition between human and computer.

Desk Set is not a prediction, rather a projection of how computer manufacturers – in this instance, IBM – wanted their machines to be perceived. Lang's film communicates a message that reinforces the virtues of technological progress, reassuring the spectator that computers were nothing to be afraid of, and that jobs would not be lost through the process of automation. Consistent with the broader message being communicated by IBM, *Desk Set* played a part in anchoring the computer's meaning with an essential presence in the workplace – the computer, in other words, as an 'International Business Machine'.

As explored in the chapters that follow, the process of ideological negotiation depicted in *Desk Set* mirrored an equivalent exchange that would later occur in the film industry, with film-makers in a range of contexts grappling with similar debates to those being experienced in the office: namely, the question of whether to adopt this technology, in the first instance, and in what precise contexts, and via which determinants, such applications might be conceived, given the limited fields and narrow range of applications generally perceived of it.

[2]

From the Scrapheap to the Science Lab: The Pioneers of Computer Animation

The history of cinema is often found in unusual places. As Thomas Elsaesser has reminded us, 'there have [always] been very distinct uses of the cinematograph and the moving image, as well as of the recording and reproducing technologies associated with them, other than in the entertainment industries' (2006, p. 20). To look beyond these industries, for Elsaesser, requires a process of 'media archaeology' (see Elsaesser, 2004, 2006; Elsaesser and Hoffmann, 1998), a reconfigured historical purview or 'expanded field' (Elsaesser, 2006, pp. 20–1) that acknowledges such alternative sites and practitioners. In keeping with this notion of parallel or parallax histories, the earliest examples of computer animation emerged far beyond those institutions and individuals more typically associated with the moving image, an alternative locale that reveals much about the digital culture of the 1950s and 1960s and the factors that determined access to the computer – still a rarefied technology, restricted to certain sectors of society, as witnessed in *Desk Set*.

In terms of closely related antecedents, brothers John and James Whitney produced films using mechanical, analogue computers, built from obsolete weapons parts discarded by the US military. Works such as *Catalog* and *Lapis* (1966, James Whitney) exist as an unexpected consequence of an expanding military-industrial complex, with the Whitneys in the role of proto-'hackers', repurposing technology originally designed for war.

Elsewhere, in the science laboratories of research and development (R&D) facilities, it was the coming together of the nascent field of computer graphics with the established demands of scientific visualisation that gave rise to the first animations produced using digital – as opposed to analogue – computers. This work was undertaken not by recognised film-makers, but by scientists and engineers. At this time, in addition to issues of access, these were the people equipped with the technical skills necessary to program and operate such complex machines.

Bell Labs was one such institution. For the research engineers who worked there – including Edward Zajac, Ken Knowlton and Michael Noll – the computer was pioneered as a tool for the animation of scientific ideas. Specifically, it was used to communicate, and in some instances generate, the results of scientific experimentation. Working frame by frame to bring movement to static graphics, research was presented in the form of animation, with the computer utilised to open up new areas of scientific enquiry and revised methods for its visualisation.

A Whirlwind of Computer Graphics

The animations produced by the Whitneys, using analogue computers, and those at Bell Labs, using digital computers, emerged from an era of expanded scientific research, an important part of the continued legacy of the military-industrial complex, which saw the computer evolve into a machine increasingly capable of sophisticated graphics, and an entire industry based on this output. The films of the Whitneys, via the scrapheap of World War II surplus, and the research engineers of Bell Labs, via the science laboratory, were intimately and inextricably linked to this context – in particular, the imaging and other devices associated with World War II and the ongoing pressures of the Cold War.

By the late 1950s and early 1960s, important developments had occurred in a range of military and related scientific contexts: from the Whirlwind designed at MIT in the early 1950s and later adopted by the US Air Force for its SAGE (Semi-Automatic Ground Environment) air defence system, the first computer capable of real-time graphics on a display (see Redmond and Smith, 2000), to Ivan Sutherland's 1962 Sketchpad (see Sutherland, 1963), an interactive design program for the creation and manipulation of geometric shapes.

The development of the display, in particular, was central to computer graphics – and, by extension, computer animation. As one example, the SAGE system – designed in the context of military command and control to detect and assist in the interception of enemy aircraft – was programmed to generate text and graphics, representing information on a screen. 'Until SAGE', proclaimed the IBM promotional film *On Guard!* (1956), produced by the company's Military Products Division, 'the miracle of the computer was its ability to calculate in split seconds and then provide printed information.' SAGE, by contrast, could translate volumes of changing data into a continuous flow of visual representation, combining speed of calculation with a capacity for visualisation. Like the radar systems on which it was founded, SAGE could model the real-time positions of aircraft, but it could also recall past representations from memory and simulate future air situations.

Crucial to the task of tracking and modelling the trajectories of aircraft, and to the later visualisations of Zajac, Knowlton and Noll, was the development of a display capable of representing such information. For the SAGE project, IBM used a large cathode-ray tube (CRT) – a device functioning in early computers as a means of storage – lit by the persistence of phosphor. 'Beyond a fantastic capacity for calculation and memory', *On Guard!* continued, 'SAGE possesses the newest and most revolutionary advance in data processing: the Displayscope.' This display represented the results of SAGE's calculations, translated into computer graphics, from which operators could select any of the on-screen 'targets' to receive additional information.

Sutherland's Sketchpad drawing program, meanwhile, was another key development in computer graphics. Introduced in 1962, using a TX-2 computer at MIT's Lincoln Laboratory, Sutherland's software functioned as part of a system that combined the CRT display and light pen (or light gun) derived from the Whirlwind and SAGE with the more general apparatus of a keyboard and control board.

While today's animation software has adopted many of the features contained within Sketchpad – including the 'rubber-banding' of lines, the drawing of scalable shapes, the use of memory structures to store objects, the zooming in and out on a display, the ability to draw perfect lines and so on – Sutherland's system was not a tool for animation, but for graphics. With Sketchpad, drawings of simple geometric shapes could be created, manipulated, duplicated and stored, with the operator employing the light pen to draw directly onto the display. He or she could see the results of this input almost immediately and make further modifications in a variety of ways.

Using systems based on the principles of computer-aided design pioneered by Sutherland, and expanding the technical apparatus of the Whirlwind and SAGE, the broader field of computer graphics flourished in the 1960s. Research laboratories adopted computers to model prototypes and simulations, with Bell Labs one of several institutions where such research was occurring – others included universities such as MIT and commercial facilities such as the Lawrence Livermore National Laboratory and Boeing Aircraft Company. At Boeing, for instance, where the term 'computer graphics' was coined by William Fetter in 1960 (see Fetter, 1965), scientists enlisted computers to produce human figure simulations, visualising adaptable representations of the human body in various aeronautical scenarios. Imagery was generated and communicated through the display, where representations could be further modified through the type of direct interaction that Sutherland described as 'man–machine communication' (1963, p. 329).

The use of the digital computer, in particular, with its distinctive imaging potential, offered new techniques for revealing and visually representing scientific data. In terms of complexity and the number of dimensions being represented, for example, it offered a number of advantages over more traditional methods of visualisation.

However, if the computer was increasingly being used for the creation of graphics, it had yet to be used to animate, to turn static images into moving images. For this, and an integrated apparatus designed for this purpose, we must turn to the scrapheap plundering of John and James Whitney, in terms of analogue computers, and the science and scientists of Bell Labs, in terms of digital variants.

From Obsolescence to Luminescence

While John Whitney, in particular, would become closely linked to the commercial film industry, having earned, as he described it, 'a reputation in professional motion picture circles as a pioneer in the development of slit-scan techniques and motion control systems' (1980, p. 29), as well as significant renown in the American avant-garde cinema (from as early as the brothers' *Five Abstract Film Exercises* [1943–4]), he and James Whitney would have to step well beyond traditional contexts and technologies in order to develop the pioneering analogue or mechanical computer systems that would play a major part in establishing this reputation. The equipment used in the production of *Catalog* and *Lapis*, for example, was initially designed and manufactured for entirely different operations, only later recycled and recon-

Brothers James and John Whitney with equipment assembled from repurposed technology

textualised – customised, adapted, combined – in fundamentally bypassing the intentionality of the original designers and manufacturers.

Specifically, the analogue computers used to produce these films were pieced together from surplus equipment disposed of by the military after World War II (for biographical information, see Moritz, 1997; Michael Whitney, 1997). Outlining this unusual lineage, John Whitney recalled how he would search through 'war surplus junk yards like an archaeologist piecing together complex machines of some other world' (1972b, p. 74). The aim, he noted elsewhere, was to adapt 'the almost worthless mechanical junk excreted from army depots across the country as the Army, Navy, Air Force, and Marines unloaded material on the surplus market' (1971a, p. 26). Such 'excretions', he added, included 'Junk such as brand new thirty-thousand-dollar anti-aircraft specialized analogue ballistic problem-solver computers dating back to World War II' (1971a, p. 26).

While digital variants of such 'obsolete' technology were increasingly prevalent, they remained beyond the reach of film-makers and other artists. As such, the Whitneys' initial interest in the relationship between cinema and computing was necessarily channelled through the salvaging of ostensibly outmoded technology. As John Whitney recalled of this surplus in a 1969 interview conducted at IBM's offices in New York, 'I began to see these things as containing within them, somehow, the possibilities for a very flexible design tool' (1970a, p. 30). Literally and metaphorically, the brothers were recycling equipment originally intended for war. In this context, it is probably no coincidence that John Whitney spoke of the computer as the artist's 'ultimate weapon' (1972b, p. 74). Like the computer hobbyists or hackers – in the original, non-pejorative sense of the word – who would later seek alternatives to officially designated functions in order to shape a computer in the vision of what Ted Nelson would later describe as 'computer lib' (1974, pp. 1–69), the Whitneys reimagined the potential uses and applications of existing tools.

Specifically, their computers were engineered from parts initially found in an M-5 (later an M-7) anti-aircraft director, part of a ballistics device developed for the guidance and control of anti-aircraft weapons. The director's intended function was to calculate the ammunition necessary to fire and hit a moving target from a particular distance. For the Whitneys, by contrast, components were converted into a device typically referred to as the 'cam machine' (John Whitney, 1970a, p. 30, for example) – a computer that performed its calculations mechanically, using a network of variable cams, among other devices, hence the name – combined with a mounted camera and used as an elaborate animation stand. Techniques and technology found parallel in the surplus parts and devices: 'Selsyn motors to interlock camera functions with artwork motions. Ball integrators to preset rate programming of some motions. And differential assemblies to control the incremental advance of the motions as each frame advanced' (1971a, p. 26). The movement of elements was mechanically computed and controlled, frame by frame, as parts previously deployed to calculate the trajectories of ballistics were transformed, as John Whitney put it, 'into devices for generating visual fluidity' (1980, p. 29).

The technologies and visual effects of *Catalog* (below), *Lapis* (opposite, top) and *Yantra* (opposite, bottom)

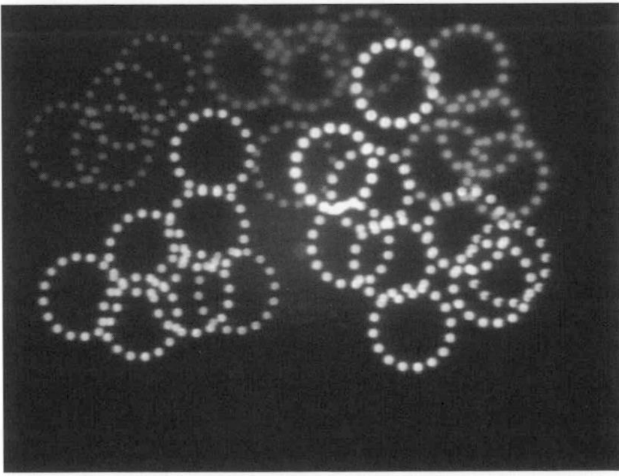

This 'visual fluidity' was at the service of Whitney's vision of 'motion graphics', describing a mode of animation that addresses 'the need for explicit *motion* in *graphics* as against the implicit motion of the painter's canvas' (1965, pp. 22–3). The distinction was between still and moving images, most obviously, but also suggests the distinctive graphics of the 'cam machine', a device John Whitney described in terms of 'trying to erect a total motion graphic system' (1965, p. 23). In combination with an optical printer – enlisted to add colour, amplify movement and apply other visual effects to the graphics, once filmed – the 'total motion graphic system' was employed to animate a series of abstract patterns and shapes.

In *Catalog* – designed as precisely that, a catalogue or showreel of visual effects that Whitney had developed and perfected through his company, Motion Graphics, Inc. – graphics in motion explode in luminescent, shimmering, cosmic abstraction. Gene Youngblood wrote of 'a brilliant display of floral patterns that seem to bloom and curl as though they were actually organic growths' (1970, p. 213), referring to the concentric forms that kaleidoscopically radiate from a central vanishing point, as if petals around a stamen. At other times, bands of colour converge and intertwine, dot patterns coalesce and disperse, and sinuous forms assemble and fragment.

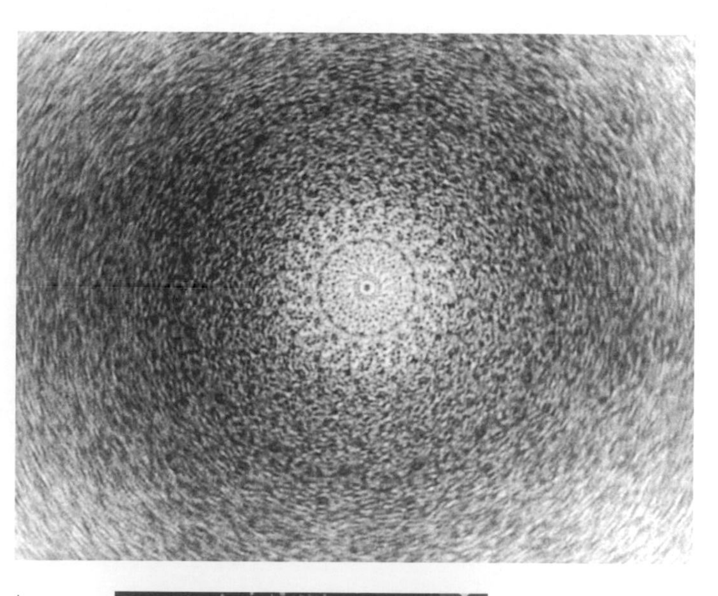

In *Lapis*, likewise, produced by James Whitney using a second 'cam machine' – indeed this was his only film created using a computer of any kind, following the hand-drawn and optically processed *Yantra* (1957), among other works – and designed as an aid to meditation, modern technology and ancient philosophy converge. On screen, in a series of slowly changing forms, mandala-like patterns swirl in a geometry of syncretic abstraction, gathering and converging, exploding and imploding, pulsing and rotating, all to the tamboura drone, tabla rhythms and sitar melody of an Indian raga.

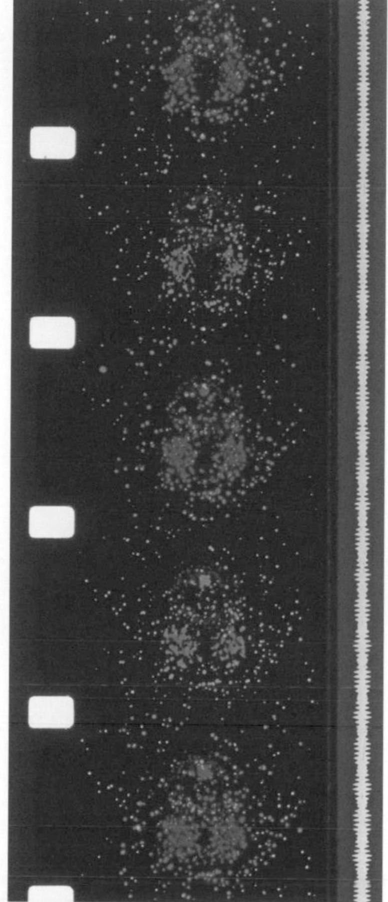

Both films, and the associated pursuit of mechanical, analogue computers at a time of transition to digital variants – at least, in certain sectors of society – point to a complex series of technological continuities and discontinuities. It was only after producing *Catalog*, for instance, that John Whitney arrived at a conscious recognition of analogue–digital parallels (see Patterson, 2009, for a detailed discussion of the relationship between the 'cam machine' and its digital equivalents, framed in relation to 'the paradigm of vision enacted by the gun controller', p. 47). 'It was only with a kind of hind-sight, a kind of delayed double take', Whitney recalled in 1968, 'that I realized I was working with a machine that was really a mechanical model of the modern digital computer graphic systems' (1972b, p. 74), adding elsewhere that it was only in retrospect that 'I began to realize that what I was doing mechanically could be done on the cathode-ray tube computer terminal' (1970a, p. 30).

As these comments reveal, the experiments of John and James Whitney spanned an extended transition – a period of overlap and parallel, as opposed to simple succession – from analogue to digital computing. Initially, as a result of the economics and broader culture of computing at this time – which saw digital machines restricted to a narrow set of sectors and professions – creative solutions were engineered far beyond the recognised contours of the commercial film and computing industries, as scrapheap junk was alchemically transformed into precious animation.

Computer Animation as R&D

At Bell Labs, meanwhile – where one would more typically expect to find the very latest technology, but not cutting-edge animation – digital variants of the Whitneys' computers were used to produce animations of a range of scientific phenomena, including the orientation of an orbiting satellite (Zajac), the use of computers as a tool for scientific visualisation (Knowlton), and the projection of three-, four-, and *n*-dimensional objects (Noll).

Computer animation was designed for the purpose of research and education, with the computer regarded as a tool for facilitating the mediation of otherwise impenetrable scientific data. Indeed if visualisation in its broadest sense is the creation of images to represent abstract information, then scientific visualisation involves the use of images, moving images and other visual forms to represent information of scientific origin or interest. Typically, as with the animations produced at Bell Labs, it deals with information the human eye cannot ordinarily see, with the purpose of either enhancing existing visuals or transforming other types of information into visual form.

What the diverse subjects depicted in these films have in common is a thematic connection with the broader field of telecommunications, in which Bell Labs' parent company, AT&T, occupied – and still occupies – a prominent position. Noll, for example, was initially appointed in 1961 to work, as he described it, 'on the subjective aspects of telephone service' (1994, p. 39), an area related to the animations he would later produce. Research into the fundamental frequency of speech data introduced Noll to the Stromberg–Carlson 4020 microfilm recorder – a device for photographing or filming the computer's display – which he initially employed to generate graphs of data pertaining to speech, but which was later central to his apparatus for computer animation. Elsewhere, Zajac's film depicted a telecommunications satellite, while Knowlton worked in the company's Computer Science Research Department, where links were forged between telecommunications and computing.

At this time, the overarching conditions at Bell Labs were conducive to fervent experimentation, often in areas only tangentially related to the development of commercial products and services. Recalling a visit to Bell Labs, Arthur C. Clarke wrote of 'the dream factory' (1958, pp. 149–57), a reference to the institution's research culture, which encompassed 'the immense range of activity and the general intellectual ferment which takes place when enough scientists are locked up together, with or without definite problems to tackle' (1958, p. 157). Able to forge their own connections with the company's broader remit, as Knowlton remembered, 'Practitioners within, tethered on long leashes if at all, were earnestly seeking enigmatic solutions to arcane puzzles' (2005a, p. 8).

Reflecting this philosophy, the umbrella of telecommunications spanned a broad spectrum of research. While the likes of Zajac, Knowlton and Noll pursued computer animation, Max Mathews – who held the title of Director of Acoustic and Behavioural Research – created the first singing computer, with the programmed rendition in 1961 of 'Daisy Bell', popularly known as 'Bicycle Built for Two', later referenced in Stanley Kubrick's *2001: A Space Odyssey*. Similarly, Billy Klüver, an electrical engineer who specialised in laser technology, participated in a number of influential art projects that required the specialist input of Bell Labs employees.

Though Zajac, Knowlton and Noll negotiated the same material and other determinants specific to Bell Labs in the 1960s, and came from broadly similar backgrounds, each had different perspectives concerning the aesthetic ramifications of their visualisations and the broader fields of computer graphics and animation. Attitudes ranged from Zajac's belief that the work produced at Bell Labs was purely scientific in nature and represented little or no aesthetic intent or interest – 'I paid zero attention to the aesthetic dimension. [...] I did not worry about art and science' (2005) – to Noll's emergent concern with the aesthetic ramifications of computer-generated still and moving images. Somewhere between these poles, Knowlton occupied a more ambivalent or fluid position, preoccupied with science, in the first instance, but a key figure in the subsequent coming together of art and technology in the later 1960s and early 1970s (see Knowlton, 1972, 1976, 2001, 2005a).

Beyond traditional conceptions of cinema, it was the principle of education that guided much of the research into computer animation as a means of scientific visualisation. 'Movies made by computer are seen to be a significant adjunct to education and scientific investigation', reported Knowlton, 'particularly in areas amenable to mathematical and logical treatment and where results can or should be visualized' (1968, p. 67). Animation, for these scientists, represented a means of augmenting and even transcending the semantic value of the written and spoken word.

Zajac, in particular, suggested that visualisation might offer an effective tool for education. 'The use of computer animation', he argued, 'for the display of the results of scientific computations is a form of education – one scientist passing information to another' (1966, p. 348). As well as the ability to see a process evolve in time, he added elsewhere, 'a movie, and particularly a perspective movie, is an important way of communicating results. Instead of the usual written report, one can even conceive of the computer making a self-contained motion picture for conveying research findings. This may have far greater impact than a verbal description' (1964, p. 169). Computer animation, in particular, was identified as an intuitive means of communicating complex principles and processes.

For Zajac, such communication might occur in the context of the classroom, as opposed to the cinema or art gallery. Outlining one potential scenario in which computer animation might be used to convey scientific ideas, he remarked:

> Suppose you are teaching a course in celestial mechanics. You want to show the satellite orbits that would result if Newton's universal law of gravitation were other than an inverse square law. On a piece of paper you write:
>
> DELT = 1.0
>
> TFIN = 1000
>
> EXP = –3
>
> CALL ORBIT (DELT, TFIN, EXP).
>
> Then you take the paper to the computation center. After a few hours, you return to pick up a movie, which you then show to the class.
>
> (1966, p. 346)

While this process would take much longer than the 'few hours' to which Zajac aspired, his broader notion of computer animation as 'a new communication medium between computers and human beings' (1967, p. 201), a tool for scientific visualisation 'both for scientists communicating with other scientists and for scientists communicating with the non-specialist' (1965, p. 1006), was consistent with the films that Zajac, Knowlton and Noll would go on to produce.

A 'Phantom Ride' through Outer Space

It was Zajac, in particular, who oversaw the first computer animation at Bell Labs, *Simulation of a Two-Gyro, Gravity-Gradient Attitude Control System*, very possibly the first created anywhere using digital computers. As he recalled, describing the film's scientific context:

> I was part of a team working on what we thought would be the first commercial telecommunications satellite system. We rejected a stationary system because, at the time, no satellite gas jet valves had survived the hard vacuum of space for more than a few months, and a stationary system would require gas jets. Instead, we opted for a medium-altitude system of thirty-six satellites in random orbits six thousand miles above the Earth, with gravity-gradient attitude control.
>
> (2005; for further details of the science depicted, see Lewis and Zajac, 1964)

Alongside more traditional techniques, the implementation of a new method for visually representing the complexities of satellite technology was integral to Zajac's project.

Scientific visualisation in *Simulation of a Two-Gyro, Gravity-Gradient Attitude Control System*

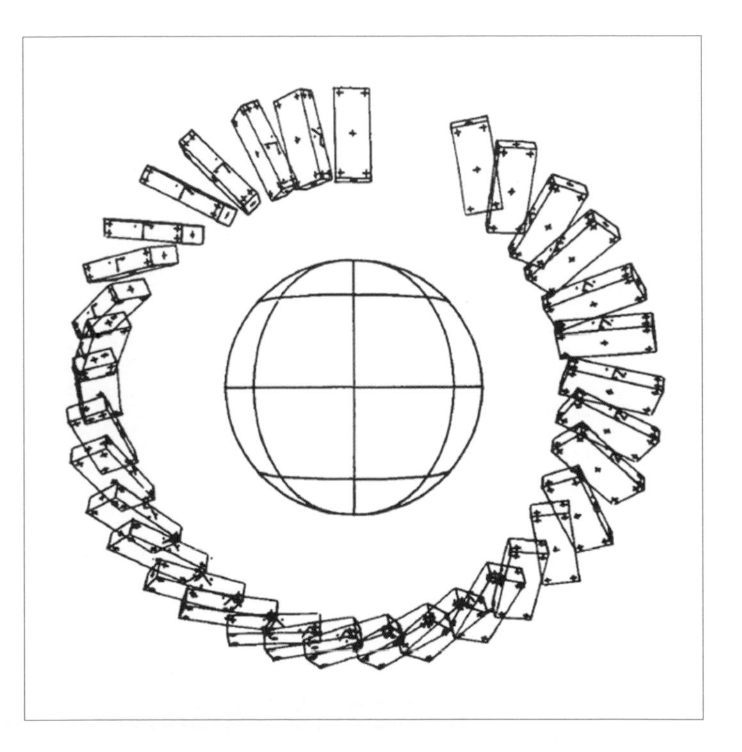

Specifically, computer animation was used to demonstrate the results of a simulation of the communications satellite's tumbling motion as a way of determining whether or not a satellite in space could be oriented and stabilised to have one of its sides, on which an antenna would be attached, constantly facing the Earth. The precise problem under consideration, noted Knowlton, was one of celestial mechanics: 'given a certain mechanism for orientation and stabilization of a communications satellite with respect to the Earth, and given certain initial conditions of insertion of the satellite into orbit, what is the satellite's resultant motion?' (1965, pp. 1117–18). For Zajac, the best way to investigate this question was through the moving image.

As the first stage of this process, while the motion of an orbiting satellite was difficult to simulate in the laboratory, its behaviour could be defined by an equation and calculated by a computer. 'It took three numbers to specify the attitude (orientation) of the satellite', Zajac explained. 'Our computer simulation produced graphs of these three numbers versus time' (2005).

Though it was relatively easy to print onto paper the numerical data concerning the satellite's orientation, the information that resulted from this process was difficult to communicate and comprehend. 'The problem of visualizing the satellite motions from the printed numbers', as Zajac described it, 'was formidable' (1966, p. 348). Printed output, he noted, would amount to 'sometimes hundreds of thousands of numbers per sheet on hundreds of thousands of sheets of paper' (1966, p. 347), material far from conducive to the effective communication of ideas concerning the simulation of a visual process. 'To construct a vivid conception of the motion out of such a table is possible but tedious' (1965, p. 282), affirmed Frank Sinden, who likewise worked on computer animation at Bell Labs, primarily in the area of simulated planetary motion (see *Force, Mass and Motion* [1965], which shows a mass under the influence of various forces). 'In the absence of a display tube or other graphical device', he wrote, 'the solution would have to be presented as a long table of angles' (1965, p. 282; for Sinden's ideas on the 'principles and programming' of computer animation, see 1967).

After some consideration, Zajac arrived at a process for replacing his countless pages of printed output, conveying instead the underlying data of one such 'table of angles' via a process of intuitive visualisation. The intention was to 'see' the results of this study rather than read them as pages of numerical data or have to manually convert this data into graphics. Accordingly, Zajac created an additional program to process the numbers that would otherwise be output as text. Numerical data was represented as a series of individual perspective drawings, which were then scanned, frame by frame, to produce animation. As he put it:

> I realized that I could write a computer program that, with the satellite represented as a brick with six identifiable sides, would visually depict the attitude motion of the satellite. I could then make runs with various parameter settings to study how best to inject the satellite into orbit and study the settling-down motion of the satellite.
>
> (2005)

This visualisation would allow Zajac to directly communicate the results of his scientific simulation, transcending more traditional methods of communicating such data.

Where pages of numerical output required significant scrutiny and specialist interpretation, the same source material could be translated into binary code and represented as moving images. 'We could readily communicate what we were finding to other members of the team' (2005), Zajac explained, identifying ease of communication as one of the major benefits of the form. From the resulting film, he noted, 'one can easily follow the motion of the satellite and the control system' (1964, p. 169), a feat 'not easily done from the inspection of plots of satellite angles versus time' (1964, p. 169).

Notably, in developing a system for performing these interconnected operations, Zajac established an early apparatus for the use of the digital computer, in particular – as opposed to the mechanical, analogue machines of John and James Whitney – as a tool for the production of moving images. At its core, an IBM 7090 (later a 7094) computer was connected to a Stromberg–Carlson 4020 microfilm recorder – originally acquired by Bell Labs 'to produce engineering graphs' (2005), according to Zajac, like those produced by Noll in his early years at the company – as a way of recording and outputting the succession of generated graphics.

The IBM 7090, introduced in 1959 and upgraded to the backward-compatible IBM 7094 in 1962, was a mainframe computer designed for performing large-scale scientific and other applications. Its input and output architecture and peripherals included the use of tape storage, punched cards, printers and other devices. While undoubtedly a sophisticated machine, what the IBM 7090 lacked, like most other computers of the time, was a display.

In conjunction, the microfilm recorder offered a means for displaying and recording computer graphics. This device consisted of an interconnected CRT (with a phosphorescent display), a camera (which could be a camera for recording still or moving images) and electronic control equipment (to instruct and maintain its operation). When fed information from the computer, the microfilm recorder converted these data into graphics, displayed on the face of the CRT, where the resulting images could be filmed. The signals for controlling the display (commands for displaying particular alphanumeric characters, spots of a certain brightness or drawing straight lines between numerically specified points) and advancing the film (recording one frame at a time, as with traditional animation) came from the electronic control equipment, which contained circuitry for reading the information sent to it by the computer, typically relayed by magnetic tape.

In terms of plotting – the charting of visual elements – the 4020 offered the type of control and speed unmatched by the human hand. 'An electronic microfilm recorder can plot points and draw lines a million times faster than a human draughtsman' (1968, p. 67), claimed Knowlton, who adopted the technological apparatus established by Zajac. In combination with the computer, he added, the microfilm recorder made 'feasible some kinds of movies which heretofore would have been prohibitively intricate, time-consuming, and expensive to draw and film' (1968, p. 67). For the scientist, computer animation was rapidly becoming a viable option, albeit through an altogether more difficult process than Knowlton's comments might suggest.

Indeed while the apparatus developed by Zajac – from the processing power of the computer to the visual plotting and integrated filming of the microfilm recorder – rendered possible a new type of visualisation, the production process remained laborious. For instance, having programmed the IBM 7090 using FORTRAN – a standard scientific programming language developed by IBM in 1957 – with instructions input via punched cards, Zajac would have to wait for his results to be processed. To compute a single minute of film at sixteen frames per second took several minutes of IBM 7090 processing time – eight minutes of computer time for one minute of film time if a rotating Earth was being depicted, or three minutes of computer time for scenes not requiring this extra computation – with the precise amount of time dependent on the complexity of representation.

Exacerbating this process, calculations were computed by batch processing, whereby computing tasks were stored up and performed together in order to maximise efficient use of a costly resource. Needless to say, this was a working method that resulted in significant delays, compounded by the additional time required to develop exposed film stock. As Zajac recalled, describing an era that preceded the widespread adoption of real-time systems:

> Everything was done by batch. I had no access to real-time computing. If I was lucky, I could get in four runs a day. With a modern PC and working in real time, I could probably do in one hour what it took me one month or more to do in the early 1960s.
>
> (2005)

The issue of real time, for Zajac, was one of convenience and speed of communication, as opposed to the intuitive creative interaction later sought by film-makers and other artists.

In terms of the content of Zajac's film, the motion of animated elements – a communications satellite, the Earth, a clock – was used to illustrate the satellite's precise position and orientation over a period of time. The satellite was drawn as a simple box – not because it particularly resembled a box, but because this was an easy shape to visualise – with plus signs serving to identify its various sides. A sphere, replete with circles of longitude and latitude, represented the Earth. The clock, meanwhile, the least complex of the graphical elements, comprised a simple representation of a clock face, which counted the number of orbits the satellite completed around the rotating Earth. Each of these elements was constructed using white lines against a black background, with the Earth shaded in some scenes through an additional process of texture mapping.

In terms of perspective, scenes were constructed from several different positions, each of which was drawn in space, as the spectator's position moved in orbit with the satellite. One viewpoint was fixed with respect to the stars, with the viewer able to see the satellite as it orbited a rotating Earth. A second viewpoint was fixed with respect to the satellite's orbit, with the viewer travelling directly behind. Like the 'phantom rides' of early cinema, where cameras were mounted on moving objects such as trains, Zajac's animation aligned the spectator with a heightened sense of movement as he or she travelled, in this instance, through a simulation of outer space.

With *Simulation of a Two-Gyro, Gravity-Gradient Attitude Control System*, Zajac demonstrated how the attitude of a communications satellite, controlled by two single-axis gyros and gravity-gradient torques, could be altered as it orbited the Earth. More generally, this study in motion led to the crystallisation of a revised apparatus for computer animation, integrating the digital computer. In the years that followed, these initial steps would be developed still further as researchers at Bell Labs and elsewhere pioneered new ways of applying this technology to the field of scientific visualisation.

Bell Flicks

If Zajac's *Simulation of a Two-Gyro, Gravity-Gradient Attitude Control System* established a digital apparatus, the work of Knowlton, on films such as *A Computer Technique for the Production of Animated Movies*, augmented these efforts, extending the range of scientific and aesthetic possibilities of computer animation. Specifically, where Zajac used FORTRAN, Knowlton sought to develop and program a new set of routines that would enable more control over the visual possibilities of the form.

As early as 1963, Knowlton enquired about the possibility of a computer language written for the specific purpose of animation. The aim, he explained, was 'Baby steps first, to see whether some simple geometric forms and text might be useful, and to see how convenient (as a language) it would be to specify simple things and motions' (2005b). Knowlton proceeded to develop a set of subroutines collectively named BEFLIX – a conflation of 'Bell' and 'flicks' – which he wrote using IBM computers (Knowlton, 1964, identifies the 7090, while 1965, 1966 and 1968, among others, refer to the 7094). Until BEFLIX, there was no standardised language or software for the production of computer animation, rather a specific set of routines programmed for each area of the process. BEFLIX integrated these operations, controlling both the computer and the microfilm recorder in generating and filming grey-scale pixel images.

A defining feature of the microfilm recorder employed by Zajac and Knowlton was its reliance on vectors, a type of graphical representation that uses straight lines to construct the outline of an object, or a series of short lines so as to give the impression of a curve. The Stromberg–Carlson 4020 was well suited to the drawing of geometrical configurations – plotting line-to-line vectors, connecting one point to another and so on – as demonstrated by *Simulation of a Two-Gyro, Gravity-Gradient Attitude Control System*. Yet, while this process convincingly simulated pen and ink and could create a certain amount of shade by densely plotting a large number of short vectors, it was not suited to filling in large areas of tone and struggled with any form of continuous shading.

With Knowlton's technique, by contrast, the application of the microfilm recorder to the creation of vectors was combined with the nuance of tonal output. The machine's display was subdivided into tiny squares – a 252-by-184 grid – each of which could be assigned one of several shades of grey, represented by a number from zero to seven, indicative of the intensity of light at that point. By using the alphanumeric character matrix contained within the microfilm recorder, letters and numbers could be variably plotted in these squares, filling the display with thousands of different characters.

Specific characters or groupings of characters were used not for any semantic purpose but to provide shading, with each character chosen for its relative brightness. 'An area of B's gives a dark shade', Zajac wrote, 'an area of commas a light shade' (1965, p. 1008). The overall effect was a mosaic of sorts, with images generated through the accumulated characters and their tonal gradations of grey. In contrast to Zajac's vector graphics, Knowlton's BEFLIX constructed images from shaded patterns and textured designs.

Like Sutherland's Sketchpad system – though lacking key elements of its interface – which introduced a series of programmed operations for the manipulation of computer graphics, BEFLIX allowed the user to determine a range of design parameters.

As Zajac explained, 'one directly varies the position and blackness of rectangular areas of the screen by means of instructions such as PAINT (paint the area a specified shade of grey), ZOOM (zoom in on the picture), DISOLV (dissolve), etc.' (1965, p. 1008). Of the functions mentioned by Zajac, 'PAINT' enabled the inside of an area drawn using vectors to be filled with a solid shade of grey; 'ZOOM' enabled all or part of an image to be enlarged; as for movement, one image could be gradually dissolved into another by selecting the 'DISOLV' command; while other features allowed the contents of an area to be moved in any direction by a controllable amount, or one area to be copied onto another and so on.

In *A Computer Technique for the Production of Animated Movies*, computer animation is itself the primary subject of the application of these techniques, produced alongside more typical scientific papers (as one example, see Knowlton, 1964, the appendices of which constitute a programmer's manual for BEFLIX, albeit unnamed in this particular article, where it is simply referred to as 'the movie language', p. 75). Throughout, fragments of text appear, collectively describing the workings of BEFLIX. 'Instructions for the desired movie enter the computer as a deck of punched cards', notes one explanatory text. 'In this new method of animation', explains another, 'both film motion and display on the tube can be controlled automatically by information on a magnetic tape.' In parallel, images of interconnected machines and their operation, outlined and shaded using the distinctive control features of BEFLIX, illustrate this process.

In this reflexive way, *A Computer Technique for the Production of Animated Movies* is as much about the potential application of the computer as a tool for the visual communication of scientific ideas as it is about any single, more general scientific principle. Knowlton's film illustrated the process of production as a means of demonstrating the potential application of the moving image to the field of scientific visualisation, acknowledging the contribution of Zajac, while foregrounding the distinctive properties of BEFLIX.

In doing so, BEFLIX expanded the range of aesthetic possibilities associated with the computer, anticipating its future role as a tool increasingly available to filmmakers and other artists – including in collaboration with Knowlton and his Bell Labs colleagues. That this was a language dedicated to computer animation, in particular, made its underlying technology more accessible to those without the programming knowledge or specialist training required to work with a general scientific language, such as FORTRAN. In the later 1960s, this would be an important part of eroding the institutional and cultural distance that restricted computer access.

3-D, 4-D and Beyond

For Noll, offering a further approach, the computer was perceived as a tool for the visualisation of multiple dimensions. 'If the computer can produce a single three-dimensional picture', he argued, 'then it also can produce a series of three-dimensional pictures to make a three-dimensional movie' (1967a, p. 75). More complexly, Noll sought to represent so-called *n*-dimensional objects, those comprising one or more dimensions beyond the familiar spatial dimensions of height, width and depth. His aim was the visual communication of a more intuitive understanding of such hyper- or *n*-dimensional objects (see Noll, 1967b). If the visual representation of such forms was not necessarily new in the mid-1960s (such objects had been researched and represented for many years – for one early printed example, see Stringham, 1880), computer animation offered new means for their simulation and visualisation. In works such as *Three-Dimensional Computer-Generated Movies*, Noll implemented this distinctive vision, suggesting in the process a revised conception of the relationship between art and technology.

Noll's approach was to use the computer to calculate and plot stereographic images, where a separate point of view is created for each eye, as a way of visualising scientific data (see Noll, 1965a, 1965b, 1967a). When viewed together stereoscopically, these images created an illusion of depth:

> A three-dimensional effect can be created by presenting two slightly different pictures separately to each eye. These two pictures are the perspective projections of some object as seen from two slightly different positions. Although the two perspectives are quite similar, the human brain translates their minute differences into a very realistic depth effect.
>
> (1965b, p. 20)

Ironically, the process for creating such imagery involved a mixture of advanced and established technology. In the first instance, Noll designed specific software for the IBM 7090 computer to calculate the data for the display of his stereoscopic projections. Having generated these co-ordinates, the computer then instructed the Stromberg–Carlson microfilm recorder to use its calculated data to generate twin plots, one for each eye, which were then filmed a frame at a time. At this point, Noll noted, 'I used one of my stereoscopes from childhood to view the images' (1994, p. 40), adopting a technology first popularised in the 1950s by the spate of 'B' and other films that exploited 3-D effects.

Noll's initial stereoscopic or 3-D animations were compiled as *Three-Dimensional Computer-Generated Movies*. 'Random Motion', for instance, depicts 3-D imagery of a geometrical object in motion, the full effect of which is only revealed when wearing stereoscopic glasses akin to those used by Noll. As the object's thirty-nine lines zig and zag, the composition as a whole transforms in evolving abstraction.

The data used to generate the object's contours and transformations were determined by a complex process of random generation, programmed by Noll and calculated by the computer. To begin with, Noll explained, the object's initial design was determined by 'sequentially connecting forty points picked at random (uniform density) to fall within a cube' (1967a, p. 76). Thereafter, 'At randomly chosen times one of the points is given a new random position within the cube, and the two lines attached to it are instantaneously twisted to new orientations' (1967a, p. 76). While random operations do not necessarily entail complexity, Noll's randomly generated animation utilised a speed of calculation distinctive to the computer.

In addition, Noll was interested in how he might adopt 3-D computer animation as a way of visually representing higher dimensions. A second piece of film, 'Rotating Four-Dimensional Hyperobject', depicts a rotating hypercube – a 4-D analogue of a cube – floating on one of its four mutually perpendicular axes. It is not a true representation of a 4-D object – a hyperobject – as Noll noted, for 'Although it is possible mathematically to specify four-dimensional objects, it is impossible to see such an object' (1967a, p. 76), as our perceptions are restricted to a maximum of three spatial dimensions. Rather, Noll's animation offered a computer simulation of a hyperobject, projected perspectively in 3-D.

Stereo pairs for three-dimensional representation in 'Rotating Four-Dimensional Hyperobject'

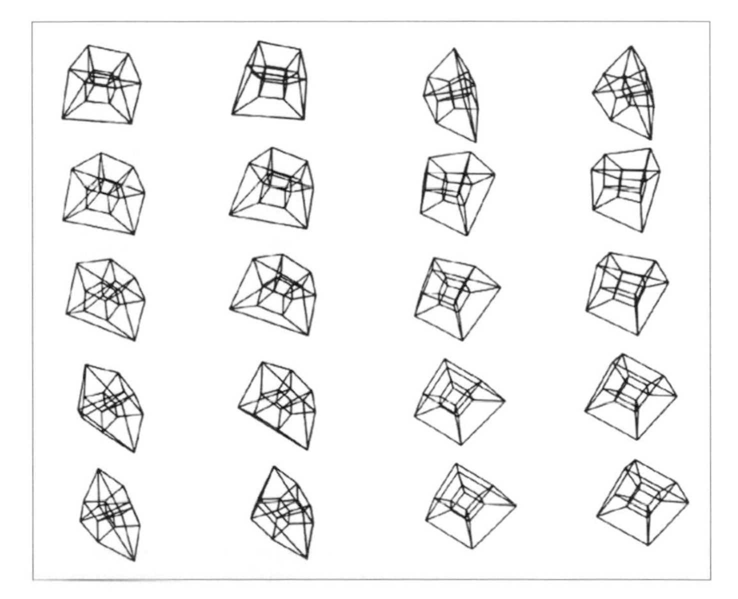

The process of performing this perspective projection, rendering visible an object whose hypothetical dimensions could be calculated but not visualised without such transformation, was necessarily difficult. The computer was used to generate the co-ordinates of the object's four dimensions, followed by the trajectory of its rotation, with the resulting orientation, as

Noll put it, 'projected down to three dimensions' (1967a, p. 76). Stereoscopic pairs were plotted, frame by frame, by the microfilm recorder, and projected through a specially designed prism adapter that used polarised glass to obtain a 3-D effect.

When rendered, this process of transformed perspectives resulted in a distinctive visual experience: a geometrically complex object that expands and contracts, moves and contorts, seemingly simultaneously in a number of dimensions. Noll, for his part, referred to the 3-D projection of a 4-D hypercube as looking like 'a three-dimensional cube within a three-dimensional cube' (1968, p. 1280, an article later reworked for the *Filmmakers Newsletter*, 1971, illustrative of increasingly connected fields), or an 'object appearing to turn inside out' (1967a, p. 76), as it rotated and transformed over time.

In contrast to Zajac and Knowlton – at least, at this particular moment – Noll readily articulated explicitly aesthetic appraisals of such work, in addition to the more typical explanations of the science being visualised. In describing his 3-D projection of a 4-D hypercube, for instance, Noll also referred to his work as 'truly a "kinetic sculpture"' (1967a, p. 76), celebrating the fact that 'Finally the computer has produced an artistic effect unattainable by any other means' (1967a, p. 76), and which, he continued, 'would probably require a lifetime' (1967a, p. 76) to attain by hand.

Meanwhile, beyond the advanced technology used to produce computer animation, or the complex mathematics involved in its 3-D representation, the visual impressions that such works elicited had the capacity to render their underlying lineage peripheral. As Noll observed of the 'Rotating Four-Dimensional Hyperobject':

> Most people, including many artists and animators, were awed by the thoroughly fascinating artistic beauty of the cube-within-a-cube that so gracefully turned itself inside out; it was purely incidental to them that the movie was produced by a digital computer or that the cube-within-a-cube was the perspective projection of a four-dimensional hypercube.
>
> (1968, pp. 1281–2)

In short, investigations into complex scientific problems could result in the type of visuals more typically associated with the conscious output of the artist.

Of those who worked with computer animation at Bell Labs, Noll was the most vocal in anticipating the convergence of fields and roles – and even produced his own computer art (see Franke, 1971, for an early survey of the field; and Noll, 1967c, for a discussion of 'the digital computer as a creative medium') – grasping the aesthetic potential of computers at a time when the majority of scientists saw little or no connection with cinema or other arts.

Yet, while Noll played an important role in pioneering new methods of computer animation, and represented an early voice in advocating an exchange between the realms of art and technology, he was also wary of collapsing the prevailing distinction between scientist and artist, in terms of their respective engagements with the computer. Expressing a degree of faith in the artist's creative vision, he wrote:

> I do feel that these techniques involving the new technology, and in particular computers, will only be exploited fully for artistic purposes when the artist who has dedicated his life to artistic explorations learns to use these new tools as new artistic media. I am an engineer and my artistic ideas are somewhat conservative. But, I am quite excited by the prospects for the new artistic effects and beauty which will surely result from creative collaboration between artists and the computer.
>
> (1968, p. 1283)

As Noll anticipated, these links would be further cultivated in the years that followed.

Conclusion

Against a backdrop of advances in computer graphics and display technology, the animations produced at Bell Labs – illustrative of a burgeoning industry in commercial R&D – extended the tools and techniques of computer animation, integrating the digital computer, in particular, as an essential technology, augmenting the antecedent apparatus of John and James Whitney. While rooted in an ostensibly scientific paradigm, as opposed to expressly artistic endeavours, experiments at Bell Labs nevertheless gave rise to a series of technical systems, aesthetic effects and broader methods and ideas that anticipated and partly facilitated the widespread use of computers by film-makers and other artists.

In terms of technology, offering an alternative to the analogue machines of the Whitneys, Zajac and others connected digital computers to the display and recording capacity of the microfilm recorder as a means of producing computer animation from static graphics.

In terms of output, dedicated programming gave rise to a series of distinctive visual modes and effects, including the vector-based motion of Zajac, the mosaic tonality of Knowlton's BEFLIX, and the random generation and higher-dimensional representation of Noll. These experiments are representative of advances in the broader field of computer animation as a form of scientific visualisation, quite distinct from the culture and concerns of Hollywood and the commercial film industry.

In terms of related discourse, these scientists contributed to historically specific debates, grappling – both in their films and accompanying papers – with the computer's fundamental characteristics. From within an explicitly scientific context, and the stated research remit of telecommunications, they nevertheless explored the purpose and potential of this machine, and the contexts and cultures in which it might operate, at a time of significant debate concerning its proper role.

Before film-makers, including John Whitney, could access such digital computers, it was scientists – one of the few groups in society who did have ready access – who were framing its creative potential, helping to establish the viability of computer animation as a vital form in the laboratory and beyond, ahead of a more conscious exchange between art and technology, artists and technologists.

In the meantime, Jean-Luc Godard's *Alphaville* would offer an altogether different vision of science and scientists, framed in terms of their intimate relationship with computers.

[3]

Tarzan vs IBM: Humans and Computers in *Alphaville* (1965)

In contrast with the Utopian perspectives on science and technology that pervaded much of the discourse concerning computers in the 1960s, Jean-Luc Godard's *Alphaville* [*Alphaville, une étrange aventure de Lemmy Caution*] explores an alternative, humanist critique of technology – albeit one necessarily realised, and therefore complicated, by the technics of cinema. With the computer's development and rapid proliferation, the notion that advanced technology might fundamentally alter our existence gained increasing currency, leading to a polarisation of perspectives, from the technophilic to the technophobic. Where the likes of Marshall McLuhan and Buckminster Fuller generally, if not always, celebrated the Utopian potential of the 'extensions of man' (McLuhan, 1964) and proposed a new 'operating manual for Spaceship Earth' (Fuller, 1969a), Godard speculated on the potentially catastrophic uses of the computer to enslave rather than liberate humanity.

Central to this vision is the projection of a technocratic state. In this sense, *Alphaville* exists as a realisation of what theorist Jacques Ellul described as 'the technological society' (1964 [originally 1954]), in which machines underpin an ideology founded on the prioritisation of technical and scientific knowledge. Extending the humanist critique of such a society – a position espoused in various hues by Ellul, Lewis Mumford (1934, 1967, 1970), Herbert Marcuse (1964, 1969) and others – Godard's film portrays the tragedy of a future in which rationality, organisation, predictability and efficiency – qualities popularly associated with the pre-personal computer – have triumphed over individuality, emotion, spontaneity and creativity.

In such a schema, the computer of *Alphaville* is defined in contrast to the very essence of humanity. Godard's film invokes what Ted Nelson described as 'the myth of "the computer"' (1974, p. 2), part of an early culture – epitomised by IBM – that sought to cloister this machine within the rarefied realms of specialist institutions, guarded over by a technical elite.

The domination of humans by the technocratic state, served and administered by a powerful computer network, becomes, for Godard, a means of interrogating the qualities that distinguish humans from computers, by way of the broader ideological and philosophical frameworks in which this relationship finds meaning. What, *Alphaville* asks, does it mean to be human? What roles are better served by machines, such as the computer? Faced with the rapid rise of computers (and the qualities associated with this technology), are humans (and humanism) ultimately doomed to obsolescence?

Such questions have been posed throughout history – not least in cinema, in representations as iconic as the dehumanising technology of Fritz Lang's *Metropolis* (1927) and Charles Chaplin's *Modern Times* (1936), which explore what it means to be human in an era dominated by machines – but assumed a renewed sense of urgency in relation to the increasingly powerful and intelligent computers of the digital age. *Alphaville* both recalls the themes of earlier films, concerned with the

Mechanised labour in *Metropolis* (below) and *Modern Times* (opposite)

dehumanised body and omnipresent machines, and extends towards the distinctive questions of consciousness and conscience evoked by the computer's rise.

The Technological Society

In negotiating the material and discursive conditions of its historical moment, *Alphaville* depicts a world in which absolute faith is placed in scientific and technical knowledge, a philosophy that finds its zenith in the form of the supercomputer Alpha 60. Secret agent Lemmy Caution (Eddie Constantine) is sent to Alphaville to rescue fellow agent Henry Dickson (Akim Tamiroff, credited as 'Akim Tamirof') and bring back or kill Professor von Braun (Howard Vernon), designer of the Alpha 60 and arch-technocrat in this city of the future. Human residents such as von Braun's daughter Natasha (played by Anna Karina, Godard's wife at the time), who Caution eventually falls in love with, have submitted to the computer's rule, subordinating their essential humanity in the process. Alpha 60, in alliance with the professor, programs and controls their existence. Natasha's position is seemingly that of many others, yet Caution sees in her, in particular, the hope of emotional salvation.

Like much of science fiction, *Alphaville* employs the appearance of a futuristic abstraction to negotiate contemporary developments and discourses. The fictional Alpha 60, for example, has revealing roots in the historical world. Most explicitly, this machine was modelled on the Gamma 60 (a connection suggested by Cournot, 1965), first announced by the Compagnie des Machines Bull in 1958 (for a detailed history, see Bataille, 1971). The Gamma 60 was seen as a large-scale processor to rival US imports – such as IBM's 705, RCA's 301 and Remington Rand's UNIVAC – from established competitors. In total, twenty units were manufactured. Customers included Électricité de France – whose headquarters and facilities feature in Godard's film as the central complex that houses the computer network's core (see Roud's introduction to Godard's screenplay, 1966, p. 10) – and the SNCF national railway.

Mass computerisation occurred against a backdrop of discourse concerning the role of the individual within society – from state policy concerning systems of governance to the intellectual shift away from existentialism, an influence on Godard, towards the structuralist movement and its general disinterest in human agency. The intertwined realms of technology and technocracy, in particular, played a major role in the modernisation of post-war France. The ascendancy of technocracy, according to Kristin Ross, 'was especially visible after 1958 when [Charles] de Gaulle consolidated his return to power surrounded by, for the first time, an elite and overt entourage of *ministres-techniciens*' (1995, p. 178), with even presidential power devolved to discrete areas of technical and in turn technological expertise.

In this context, in functioning as a symbol of centralised reason and control, Alpha 60 illustrates the complex relationship that exists between technology, the computer as material embodiment, and technocracy, an ideological system that often utilises machines but is not necessarily predicated on their application. Although intimately related, technology and technocracy are neither synonymous nor mutually dependent. For Ellul, 'the machine is the most obvious, massive, and impressive example of technique, and historically the first' (1964, p. 3), but it is not the only one. In the context of the mid-twentieth century, he argued, 'Technique has now become almost completely independent of the machine, which has lagged far behind its offspring' (1964, p. 4). This larger phenomenon, technique – '*la technique*' in Ellul's original – consists of 'nothing more than *means* and the *ensemble of means*' (1964, p. 19), the collective principles, impulses and workings of *all* individual techniques, which are used to achieve any end whatsoever, whether by machine or otherwise.

What Ellul described as 'the technological society' is dominated by logic, the technical pursuit of which becomes an end in its own right; and, in the case of technocracy, an explicitly articulated ideology – one quite distinct from Ellul's own brand of humanism, rooted in religious thinking. Such a society is founded on technique, technicians, technicism and, as an extension of these expressions, the more traditional understanding of technology as physical tools or machines. In all aspects of life, human impulses are necessarily redirected into expressions and behaviours that are more deliberate and rationalised, with citizens transformed into dehumanised components of a larger technical system.

Ellul was not alone in warning of such a scenario. Mumford, likewise, described a society increasingly seen as taking on the qualities of machines – though this was a process, he argued, that had been occurring for hundreds of years. 'Within the last four centuries', he wrote, 'the older tradition of polytechnics', which enlists many different modes of technology as a framework for solving human problems, 'was replaced by a system that gave primacy to the machine, with its repetitive motions, its depersonalized processes, its abstract quantitative goals' (1970, p. 164). This new system, which he termed 'technics' (see 1934, 1967, 1970), was based on technology for its own sake, as opposed to human utility.

The world portrayed by Godard exists as a fictional variation of Mumford's 'technics' and Ellul's 'technological society', in which Alpha 60 and Professor von Braun have conditioned the population to deny the existence of human freedom. As Caution enters the city, he is greeted with a sign – 'ALPHAVILLE. SILENCE. LOGIC. SAFETY. PRUDENCE' (here and elsewhere, translations are from Peter Whitehead's English version of Godard's screenplay, 1966) – that offers an appropriate credo for a society maintained by a multitude of technical processes. The city is split into two zones, North and

Supercomputer Alpha 60 as a tool for interrogation

South, the climates of which are carefully maintained, so that one produces perpetual sun, the other perpetual snow. No parameter of Alphaville's existence, not even the weather, extends beyond the harness of science and technology.

The movements of residents are also carefully monitored by the state, with numbers imprinted onto the bodies of certain individuals as a way of collapsing identity into numerical data, more easily stored and monitored by the computer. Ironically, this function mirrors the intended use of the initial purchase of the first commercially available digital computer, the UNIVAC, by the US Census Bureau in 1951 (for a general history of computing, see Campbell-Kelly and Aspray, 2004; Ceruzzi, 2003). 'People have become slaves to probability', Caution laments, to which Dickson responds, 'Here at Alphaville their ideal is ... a pure technocracy ... an entirely technical society ... like those of ants and termites!' In the same way that the joyous shifts of changing seasons are replaced by meteorological monotony, individual expressions are outlawed, banned for being both irrational and inefficient.

Scientists and mathematicians, by contrast, are deified as the embodiment of technical expertise. Such figures are memorialised in the naming of streets – at one point, Caution is directed to 'Heisenberg Boulevard, on the corner of Mathematics Park' – and mathematical formulae, such as Albert Einstein's $E=mc^2$, are intercut throughout the film. In this way, Godard emphasises the primacy of science and mathematics as defining discourses, visually punctuating the film's action with the precise rationale for the world we have entered, in which individual conscience is sublimated by a collective faith in elite technicians.

While the likes of Ellul saw the technological society as 'a universal concentration camp' (1964, p. 427), a view seemingly shared by Godard, others pointed to the progressive potential of advanced technology, including the computer, as a means of addressing the world's major problems. Fuller proposed a new harmony between technology and the Earth's ecology. 'Man is going to be displaced altogether as a specialist by the computer' (1969a, p. 44), he noted, recalling the argument espoused by Ellul, but with an altogether different end result. Elsewhere, he added:

> The computer is an imitation human brain. There is nothing new about it, but its capacity, speed of operation, and tirelessness, as well as its ability to operate under environmental conditions intolerable to the human anatomy, make it far more effective in performing special tasks than is the skull and tissue encased human brain, minus the computer.
>
> (1969a, pp. 112–13)

Given these qualities, he suggested, demonstrating a degree of faith in the progress of technology, 'all politicians can and will yield enthusiastically to the computers [sic] safe flight-controlling capabilities in bringing all of humanity in for a happy landing' (1969a, pp. 132–3), a scenario that stands in stark contrast to the catastrophe – or crash landing, to extend Fuller's metaphor – depicted in *Alphaville*.

McLuhan, likewise, often in opposition to those who sought to critique advanced technology, saw the computer and other modern electronic media as pivotal tools. 'The computer', he and Quentin Fiore argued, 'is by all odds the most extraordinary of all the technological clothing ever devised by man, since it is the extension of our central nervous system' (1968, p. 35). The computer was perceived as an amplification of humanity, as opposed to a means of suppressing the essentially human. Although this position can and has been critiqued (as one early example, see Rosenthal, 1968), McLuhan's ideas – and their reception, where ambiguity and complexity were often overlooked in favour of evangelical zeal – remain useful in revealing the Utopian rhetoric of this period.

While there is no evidence to suggest that Godard was directly aware of the writings of Mumford, Ellul, Fuller or McLuhan, *Alphaville* nevertheless explores the fundamental merits or otherwise of a world increasingly rooted in technics, technocracy and the technological society.

The Computer as Technocratic Tool

Alpha 60, in particular, is the symbolic locus for this exploration, with the material tools that sustain such a society central to its workings. In Godard's fiction, the computer both implements and perpetuates von Braun's regime. Comprising 1.4 billion nerve centres, it is, Dickson describes, 'a giant computer … like the ones we used to have, you know? […] IBM […] Olivetti … General Electric […] Alpha 60 is the same, but a hundred and fifty light years stronger'. This processing power is used to dictate every parameter of existence. The computer calculates and programs the everyday lives of the population, applying scientific and technical thinking to instil and maintain order, founded on the notion that such principles can lead to a more efficient society than can otherwise be achieved.

In visual terms, Alpha 60 and its networked nodes are most frequently represented through an abstraction, a visual binary created by a recurring flashing light that functions as proxy signification. The dark streets of the city, depicted by celebrated cinematographer Raoul Coutard, sharply contrast with the blinding lights of the electronic nerve centres, whose intermittent flashing exercises a hypnotic spell.

This blinking – on, off; a corollary of binary code – gives presence to the sprawling machine.

While real computer hardware of the time – whirring magnetic tape, racks of wired components, control panels and so on – is revealed when Caution tours the Control Centre that houses the inner workings of Alpha 60, Godard's favoured representation of the computer is deliberately archaic. 'By representing a computer advanced enough to wage atomic war on the world with a single lamp', Harun Farocki has noted in highlighting this paradox, '*Alphaville* signals its allegiance to those low-budget films in which an ordinary table plate designates a single flying saucer' (Silverman and Farocki, 1998, p. 59). The power of the machine is signified through its seeming omnipresence, as opposed to sophisticated architecture.

In terms of the film's soundtrack, the pervasiveness of Alpha 60 – both its voice and electronic emissions can reach any citizen, any time, in any part of the city – is signified through a number of sonic devices. At the Control Centre, the computers whirr. Elsewhere, Alpha 60's flashing light is accompanied by a Morse code-like electronic bleep. The computer's spoken voice, meanwhile, is typically dissociated from any apparent source. It becomes an ethereal presence, permeating the world as a sonic signifier of the ruling technocracy. In terms of timbre, the voice is distressed and distorted. Ironically, this seemingly synthetic voice was provided by a human, a man who had lost his voice-box and learned to speak again. According to Richard Roud, in introducing Godard's screenplay, the director 'thought it was important to have, not a mechanical voice, but one which has been, so to speak, killed' (Godard, 1966, p. 16). Emblematic of the film as a whole, Alpha 60 exists as the corollary of a loss of consciousness.

The computer slaves tirelessly, calculating the permutations, probabilities and parameters of its society, their mathematical underpinnings and the individual's role within the larger whole. 'One must not be afraid of logic', Caution is instructed. 'The function of Alpha 60', he discovers, 'is the prediction of the data which Alphaville obeys', a description in keeping with Godard's original notion, as outlined in his treatment, of a machine 'whose work consists in recording in its thousand memories the behaviour of everybody and everything, [...] with tasks like the departure of trains and aeroplanes, the traffic, the distribution of electricity, the repression of crime, etc.' (1966, pp. 92–5). After all, Caution hears, 'In the life of all individuals, as well as in the lives of nations themselves, everything is determined by cause and effect.' The implication is that just as a powerful computer might calculate the organisation of society, so too might it determine the interior life of each individual.

In this sense, though not fully developed or articulated – certainly not to the extent of later films such as Stanley Kubrick's *2001: A Space Odyssey*, which *Alphaville* anticipates – Alpha 60 embodies a degree of intelligence. Not only does this machine implement the technical systems designed by Professor von Braun, it also learns by performing complex calculations and analysing their output. The society of Alphaville, Caution notes, 'has developed itself at lightning speed, by following the orders of its electronic brains, which at the same time have developed themselves by creating problems beyond the range of the human mind'. Through such methods, implemented at the Control Centre, Alpha 60 predetermines the conditions of existence. The machine controls transport, the supply of electricity, military operations, and even the movement of goods and people, identifying the most efficient techniques for maintaining each of these elements and their relation to the workings of society.

When it dawns on Alpha 60 that its capabilities have transcended the technical potential of the human brain, the logical ramification of this evolution is the computer's subjugation of its human progenitors. Yet, Alpha 60 points to a higher order, the self-perpetuating pursuit of ever greater technique – *à la* Ellul's technological critique – as the ultimate rationale for this *coup d'état.* Alpha 60 asserts:

> Do not believe that it is I ... who elicits this destruction ... nor the scientists who have accepted the plan. Ordinary men are unworthy of the position they occupy in the world. An analysis of their past draws one automatically to this conclusion. Therefore they must be destroyed, which is to say, transformed.

In resisting this scenario, the computer argues, humanity denies its logical and therefore inevitable subordination.

This process of 'transformation', the creation of a world akin to the technological society that Ellul and others feared was emerging in the historical world, suggests a fundamental loss of humanity to the computer's rational logic. For Ellul, humans were already becoming more like machines, manifesting '*l'homme-machine*' (1964, p. 395), a dehumanised entity that epitomises this loss of agency. Under Alpha 60's direction, humanity is effectively mechanised, with individuals programmed to behave as machines.

Expressions of love, for example, are alien to the computer and are therefore outlawed. The capacity to love is not only a distraction to ordered existence, but is actively forbidden, to the point where the very notion has been forgotten. 'No one ever falls in love with you?', Caution asks of Natasha, to which she replies, 'In love? What's that?' Dickson, meanwhile, in his dying throes, is unabashed in his expressions, courting his erotic partner with amorous platitudes, spoken in several languages. Yet, this exchange is rendered deviant, an act of prostitution. In Alphaville, Dickson can proclaim his love, but only as an illicit fetish, a perversion serviced by a professional seductress.

Elsewhere, the computer's rule determines which words are listed in an evolving dictionary, referred to as 'the Bible', which is placed in every room and pored over with the type of reverence typically reserved for religious texts. This semantic control results in the banishment from consciousness of a series of words – including 'conscience' and 'why' ('one never says "why", but "because"', admonishes one engineer), which suggests a questioning of existence, in general, and the ideological underpinnings of society, in particular, as well as 'redbreast', 'to weep', and 'tenderness', which convey emotion – that are deemed antithetical to the logic of scientific and technical control. Words disappear nearly every day as part of this regulated lexicon, replaced by others more in keeping with the technocratic regime, while armed guards watch over the Institute of General Semantics, with language deployed as an ideological weapon.

Ironically, not only is centralised rule shared between the alliance of von Braun and Alpha 60 – the machine itself does not govern, though its calculations are obeyed by the residents of Alphaville – this control is largely the result of consensual submission, albeit in the face of sometimes brutal oppression. 'Outsiders have been assimilated wherever possible [...]', Caution reports. 'The others, who could not adapt, were purely and simply put to death.' The majority of residents submit willingly to, or are unable to resist, the advances of this society.

Ellul described such individuals, in the historical world, 'who have so completely renounced the inner life as to hurl themselves gladly and without regret into a completely technicized mode of being' (1964, p. 411), as examples of the 'joyous robot' (1964, p. 411). Under the computer's rule, calculations serve to determine efficient systems that keep the population employed, fed and clothed. These 'joyous robots' have everything they could wish for – except, of course, their freedom.

Those who resist face a weary existence, perennially on the run from Professor von Braun and the omnipresent Alpha 60, a machine that sees, hears and pinpoints those who contest its authority. Enrico Fermi, a bastion for poetry, is a hideout for those who resist the state. Suicide, for many, becomes the only alternative to the regime. Others are apprehended and executed in elaborate public rituals, shot on a swimming pool's diving board, then stabbed to death by a team of synchronised executioners who conduct their capital punishment in water, to the polite applause of those who gather to witness and condone this punitive spectacle. The crimes of those who are executed? They are deemed to have 'behaved illogically', as one technical expert puts it; that is, to have resisted the fundaments of the technological society.

Yet, even in the face of execution, some resistors remain steadfast, articulating the type of humanist critique espoused by Ellul and others. 'In order to create life, it is merely necessary to advance in a straight line towards all that we love', cries one

– a refrain repeated by Natasha near the film's climax as her own emotions are aroused – moments before he is executed for grieving the death of his wife. 'We see the truth that you no longer see', beseeches another. 'This truth is, that there is nothing true in man except love and faith, courage and tenderness, generosity and sacrifice' – qualities defined in opposition to those of Alpha 60.

The Myth of the Computer

Godard's working title for *Alphaville*, 'Tarzan vs IBM', points explicitly to the symbolic opposition between humans and computers, a polarisation drawn between heroic humanity, exemplified by the primitivism of Tarzan, on the one hand, and the predominant force in the 1960s computing industry, IBM, on the other. Where Tarzan once fought the perils of the jungle (in countless novels, films and television series following Burroughs's original, 1914), Caution now battles the dehumanising forces of Alphaville, going head to head with Alpha 60 and the technological society it underpins. The Paris of the 1960s is transformed into the futuristic jungle of Alphaville's cityscape, with Alpha 60, in Godard's original treatment, 'a type of machine one hundred thousand times more perfect but analogous in principle to the computers already in use [...], in companies like IBM, General Electric, etc.' (1966, p. 87).

IBM, in particular, is implicitly positioned as the equivalent of the elite technicians of Alphaville, with their computers the collective corollary of Alpha 60. The reputation of IBM in the 1960s, as Ted Nelson has noted – arguing in 1974 in favour of a shift towards personal computing – was one of guarded hegemony, a collective of programmers, engineers, operators and other experts who controlled access to their machines. In making his plea for 'computer lib' (1974, pp. 1–69), Nelson went so far as to describe the global computer giant as 'Big Brother' (1974, p. 52), the 'International Brotherhood of Magicians' (1974, p. 52), part of the 'computer priesthood' (1974, p. 2) and even the 'Institute of Black Magic' (1974, p. 52), remonstrating that computers were being unnecessarily mythified by those who worked at IBM.

This myth, to which Godard's film contributes, portrays the computer as symbolically opposed to humanity. 'Man has created the myth of "the computer"', Nelson explained, 'in his own image, or one of them: cold, immaculate, sterile, "scientific", oppressive' (1974, p. 2). He argued:

> Public thinking about computers is heavily tinged by a peculiar image which we may call the Myth of the Machine. It goes as follows: there is something called the Machine,

> which is Taking Over The World. According to this point of view The Machine is a relentless, peremptory, repetitive, invariable, monotonous, inexorable, implacable, ruthless, inhuman, dehumanizing, impersonal Juggernaut, brainlessly carrying out repetitive (and often violent) actions.
>
> (1974, p. 9)

Battling the white-coated technocratic elite of *Alphaville*

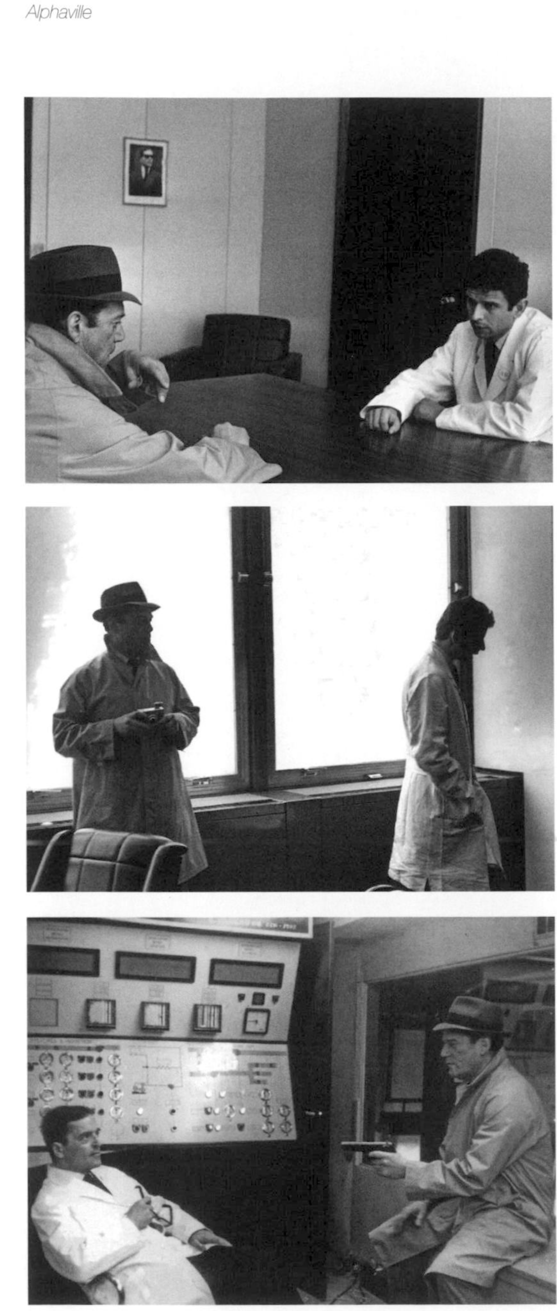

Elsewhere, a defence of computers posited by J. C. R. Licklider begins by outlining the same myth:

> For many, the computer is a cold, precise machine that lives behind a glass wall, a machine intolerant of the slightest error in the thick decks of punched cards it receives, indifferent to the reading habits of those to whom it presents great stacks of printout paper full of capital letters, and on the whole best dealt with not more often than once a day, and then through its retinue of intermediaries – its programmers, keypunch operators, dispatchers, computer operators, and field engineers.
>
> (1968, p. 275)

Although the descriptions by Nelson and Licklider refer to the computers of the historical world – and historically specific perceptions of these machines – they might just as well be describing the fictional Alpha 60, with its white-coated programmers and myriad engineers, the equivalent of the technical experts whose status is elevated to a shadowy elite in Ellul's 'technological society'. Where Nelson conceptualised the computer as a 'dream machine' (1974, pp. DM1–DM59), which might take on as many forms and functions as the human imagination could conceive, the computer of

Alphaville is monolithic, the material manifestation of the ideology that gave rise to it, and which it now perpetuates.

Poetry, in particular, is portrayed as the epitome of human expression – again, defined in contrast to the computer – a means of reclaiming language in a society of overwhelming semantic control. Poetry, a form both expressive and affecting, offers the exquisite crystallisation of emotion. Indeed, it is poetry – Paul Éluard's *Capitale de la douleur* [*Capital of Pain*] (1926) – that the fading Dickson hands Caution as a weapon (for a detailed study of Godard's use of Éluard's poetry, see Darke, 2005; Martin, 2004). We see several scenes of Caution reading from this text, and it is Éluard's words, coupled with Caution's expressions of love, that eventually rouse Natasha from her emotional slumber.

In terms of related discourse, Marcuse outlined his own critique of a society in which technology functions to dehumanise, the antithesis of poetry and other forms of art, which he took to represent freedom. His ideal, addressing a sense of entrapment not specific to technology – though technology was identified as a contributing factor in the creation of 'one-dimensional man' (1964) and a society enslaved despite its apparent prosperity (1969) – was a world in which art is so fully integrated with existence that the two are impossible to separate:

> The liberated consciousness would promote the development of a science and technology free to discover and realize the possibilities of things and men in the protection and gratification of life, playing with the potentialities of form and matter for the attainment of this goal. Technique would then tend to become art, and art would tend to form reality: the opposition between imagination and reason, higher and lower faculties, poetic and scientific thought, would be invalidated.
>
> (1969, p. 24)

This idealistic vision stood in stark contrast to what Marcuse saw as the loss of freedom to industrial society, which was in turn at the service of capital. 'The industrial society which makes technology and science its own', he wrote, 'is organized for the ever-more-effective utilization of its resources' (1964, p. 17). Meanwhile, describing the type of logic paralleled by the rule of Alpha 60, he noted how 'the technological controls appear to be the very embodiment of Reason for the benefit of all social groups and interests – to such an extent that all contradiction seems irrational and all counteraction impossible' (1964, p. 9).

In *Alphaville*, according to the binary opposition at work in the historically specific myth concerning the computer, the essentially human, in contrast to this machine, is identified most explicitly in the capacity to feel, the emotive expressions of language, the ideological and metaphysical questioning of existence and acts of impulse and desire.

Humanity in the 'Capital of Pain'

Ultimately, the distinction that *Alphaville* draws between human and computer is located in the related realms of consciousness and conscience. By exploiting fundamental differences in these areas, Caution triumphs over Alpha 60 and Professor von Braun, destroying Alphaville in the process.

This climax is anticipated by Caution's interrogation by Alpha 5, one of Alpha 60's complex of computer units. He is asked a series of probing, abstract questions – 'What transforms the night into the day?', 'What is your religion?', 'Is there a difference between the mystery of the laws of knowledge and those of love?' – designed to function as an ideological evaluation. It is 'poetry', Caution responds, that illuminates the night; his religion, we discover, is based upon 'immediate inspirations of my conscience'; while love, in contrast to the principles of knowledge, is regarded as 'no mystery'.

The 'capital of pain' and the redemptive power of poetry

This defence of poetry, conscience and love amounts to a direct challenge to the ideology of Alphaville. Indeed, this scene reveals the core of a humanist critique – a manifesto of sorts, which outlines the qualities and expressions that exemplify the essence of humanity and offer a means of resistance to its proposed subordination – of the parallel societies of Alphaville, most obviously, in terms of fiction, and the increasingly technological society of Paris, in the historical world, by implication and refraction.

Like those who were executed, Caution renounces the society that uses computers to constrain humanity. 'I do refuse to become what you call normal', he decries. This humanist position is expressed less equivocally in another of Caution's conversations with the computer. 'You can go and stuff yourself with your bloody Logic!', he remarks at one stage, a sentiment that might equally encapsulate the various positions of Ellul, Mumford or Marcuse. When the computer orders Caution to consent to form part of 'a superior race ... to normal men' or be 'eliminated', a scenario described as being 'for the Universal Good', the secret agent unleashes his most powerful weapon.

This 'secret', as Caution terms it, is an enigmatic riddle that points to the core of humanity as the means for the ultimate destruction of Mumford's 'technics', Ellul's '*la technique*' and so on. The answer, which exists beyond the circuitry of any computer, is described as 'Something that never changes with the night or the day, as long as the past represents the future, towards which it will advance in a straight line, but which, at the end, has closed in on itself into a circle.' If, Caution continues, the computer were ever to realise the riddle's answer, which it does by the close of the film, 'you will destroy yourself in the process ... because you will have become my equal, my brother'. In other words, computers such as Alpha 60, 'who are not born ... do not weep ... and do not regret', will either cease to function, having achieved the inspiration of conscience that Caution defines as his religion, or implode in denial as the ultimate expression of the computer's internal logic, short-circuiting as it thinks like a human in order to solve the riddle.

Having dealt with Alpha 60, Caution next confronts Professor von Braun, denouncing the technician who perfected this machine. 'You are opposing my moral and even supernatural sense of vocation, with nothing more than a physical and mental existence created and dictated by technocracy', he explains, before killing the arch-technocrat. 'Such people', Caution continues, 'will serve as terrible examples to all those who use the world as their theatre, where technical power and its religion become the Rules of the Game.'

One of the film's most significant scenes sees the ultimate stirring of Natasha's resistance to this technical power and its technological manifestation. The antidote to this world exists in the redemptive power of poetry, which is further represented as the quintessence of human impulses and endeavours. Through Éluard (lines such as '*Nous vivons dans l'oubli de nos metamorphoses* [...]/*Mais cet écho qui roule tout le long du jour*/*Cet écho hors du temps d'angoisse ou de caresses* [...]/*Sommes-nous près ou loin de notre conscience*' [though Natasha is seen reading *Capitale de la douleur*, these lines are from 'Notre mouvement', *Le dur désir de durer*, 1946], translated by Whitehead as 'We live in the void of our metamorphoses [...]/But that echo that runs through all the day/That echo beyond time, despair and the caress [...]/Are we close to, or far away from our conscience'), Caution stirs in Natasha the human qualities she has all but forgotten in the course of assimilation. In undoing this process, Caution teaches Natasha the meaning of the words 'conscience' and 'love'. Via Éluard ('*Il suffit d'avancer pour vivre*/*D'aller droit devant soi*/*Vers tout ce que l'on aime*' [this time from 'La petite enfance de Dominique', a poem about Éluard's wife, *Le phénix*, 1951]), she echoes the refrain of the executed resistor – in Whitehead's translation, 'One need only advance to live, to go/Straightforward towards all that you love' – and, as she takes tentative steps towards a new lexicon of redemptive humanity, she offers her own utterance: 'I … love … you …'.

Through the humanising power of emotion, Natasha is transformed into someone who is free to think and feel; to be, in other words, human. The destruction of Alphaville, whose inhabitants are stricken in a swoon of despair, is signified by the flickering oscillation between positive and negative imagery, an effect that recalls the flashing light of Alpha 60. In the face of the dehumanising impulse of technocracy, aligned with the processing power of the computer, this threat is defused by one simple phrase – 'I love you' – that the machine, in this mythologised representation, can never understand.

Conclusion

At a time of renewed faith in the technological society, facilitated by the computer's proliferation and associated ways of thinking and being, *Alphaville* brought into focus the fundamental question of how we reconcile, if at all, the respective qualities associated with humans and computers. Only through emotion and creative inspiration, Godard's film suggests, can human beings make intellectual and spiritual progress; without this element of humanity, we too are machines.

Although not typically thought of as a humanist, and necessarily implicated in technics by virtue of his profession – a complex relationship with technology that recurs throughout the director's career – Godard admonished a world in which those who are 'beyond codification' (1966, p. 95), evoking the terminology associated with the transmutation of the world into the underlying binary language of the digital computer, are deemed illogical, aberrant and in need of assimilation.

This dystopian theme of humanity being dominated by machines is not necessarily new, of course; the notion of intelligent machines that transcend the computational power of the human brain has been explored in numerous films and continues to be a staple of science fiction, while the universal nature of the conflict between humans and machines is implicit in Godard's reference to Tarzan's fantasy battle with IBM, played out by Caution and Alpha 60.

Yet, Godard's exploration of the relationship between humans and machines is also framed according to the distinctive symbolic presence of the computer and its evolving status at a particular historical juncture. This technology provided a variation on the theme of humanity's subjugation by machines. In reworking this notion for the digital age, *Alphaville* revealed the Gamma 60 – in its refracted guise of the fictional Alpha 60 – to be a source of considerable threat at a time when the computer was perceived by many as bringing us one step closer to a soulless technocracy. In projecting this inversion of the typical master–slave relationship, Godard's film reveals as much about the specific context of the mid-1960s as it does about the future era it ostensibly depicts.

Specifically, in magnifying contemporary attitudes and anxieties, *Alphaville* resonates with the philosophical discourse of the time, negotiating through sound and image the ideas central to the humanist critiques of technology espoused by Ellul, Mumford, Marcuse and others, while arriving at Godard's own distinctive position. The director emerges as a resistor to blind faith in technology, not unlike the dissident poets of his fictional future, but one who draws on the expressive potential of cinema, a form necessarily rooted in technology. The Paris of the 1960s becomes the 'capital of pain', a society of technological alienation, which can only be saved through a renewed faith in love, poetry and individual liberty – qualities, for Godard, that are antithetical to the computer as technocratic tool, but are not beyond the technics of cinema. This tension between cinema and technology, art and industry, was one that would soon be addressed by the broadly contemporaneous experiments of the art and technology movement.

[4]

Digital Harmony: The Art and Technology Movement

Let's get together somehow.

Stan VanDerBeek on the realms of art and technology (*Stan VanDerBeekiana*, 1968, Nick Havinga, for the CBS television series *Camera Three*)

All these potentialities lay before me [...]. A question remained: What computer, whose computer?

John Whitney on the 1960s and his search for access to powerful computers (1980, p. 30)

In stark contrast to the vision of science and scientists and the myth of the computer – as a cold, sterile machine, in direct contrast to the human capacity for emotion and poetry – propagated by Jean-Luc Godard's *Alphaville*, it was precisely such technologists to whom film-makers and other artists turned in the mid-1960s. Via specialist engineers, access increased to the facilities of universities and commercial research laboratories – including at IBM, in an ironic twist on the mythical battle implied by Godard's working title, 'Tarzan vs IBM'. More than a decade after the launch of the first commercially available digital computers, collaboration with scientists finally saw film-makers adopt such machines, integrating their creative visions with a defining technology of the day.

Of the collaborations initiated at this time, two stand out for their aesthetic explorations and reflexive investigations of the coming together of cinema and computing. At Bell Labs, following the scientific visualisations of Edward Zajac, Ken Knowlton, Michael Noll and others, experimental film-maker Stan VanDerBeek teamed up with Knowlton to develop new computer animation techniques that might one day be applied to the field of telecommunications, in which Bell's parent company, AT&T, occupied a prominent position. At IBM, meanwhile, mirroring this grouping of artist and technologist, research engineer Jack Citron worked with abstract animator John Whitney to investigate the graphics potential of a new computer, the IBM System/360 Model 75, and its display unit, the IBM 2250.

This culture of collaboration reflected a broader commitment to communication between artists and technologists. The art and technology movement, as it was known, which flourished in the mid- to late 1960s, offered a new model for collaboration, pairing the creative vision and aesthetic concerns of the artist, on the one hand, with the scientific knowledge and technical expertise of the technologist, on the other (for an early account of these activities, see Davis, 1973). A philosophy of working together, it was believed, would provide a modus operandi capable of exploring the pressing concerns of a society thoroughly imbued with technology, including the computer, and a symbolic model for its productive application in all sectors of society.

If Whitney would go on to write at length about 'digital harmony' (1980), he did so as a means of illuminating a phenomenon quite distinct from the context of collaboration in which this notion might also function as the perfect metaphor. Where, for Whitney, 'digital harmony' referred to 'the complementarity of music and visual art' (1980) – with abstract animation, in particular, formally analogous to visualised music – the collaborations of the art and technology movement might also be understood in terms of harmonics. After all, a version of 'digital harmony' was precisely what was sought by the likes of VanDerBeek and Whitney – in this context, a symbiotic relationship with technologists and their computers.

The Computer as Collaborative Tool

The experiments of VanDerBeek and Knowlton, at Bell Labs, and Whitney and Citron, at IBM, reflected a changing technological environment. Alongside the computer's continued proliferation, one might also point to the dawning of the space age and the development of global satellite telecommunications as momentous events. At the same time, this era also gave rise to an equally intense discourse – a concomitant acceleration in awareness, understanding and ideas – concerning the status of technology and its potential to shape the future. While critiques of this new environment were not unknown, a more prevalent response espoused a radical faith (see Fuller, 1969a; McLuhan, 1964), an intellectual current that emerged at a time when technology was taking on reconfigured meaning with regard to human experience.

In the realm of art, in particular, as the potential impact of technology was foregrounded, film-makers and other artists sought to participate more actively in increasingly technological times. 'Society is in a state of enormous transition', wrote Roy Ascott, in one of the first articles of the period to explicitly advocate awareness and engagement. 'The most extensive changes in our environment can be attributed to science and technology. The artist's moral responsibility demands that he should attempt to understand these changes' (1964, p. 38). The natural creative response, affirmed critic Douglas Davis, was to turn 'to the products, processes and imagery of science and technology' (1968, p. 29). Elsewhere, Gene Youngblood noted the need for a revised aesthetic, rooted in technology, as a way of expressing a new subjectivity. 'Aesthetic application of technology', he proffered, 'is the only means of achieving new consciousness to match our new environment' (1970, p. 189), an engagement that would require a major shift in focus.

Attempts to respond to the context outlined by Ascott, Davis, Youngblood and others took many forms, with collaboration one of several models that emerged. Others included 'intermedia', a term coined by Fluxus artist Dick Higgins (see 1966), and its moving-image equivalent, 'expanded cinema', described by Sheldon Renan as

> cinema expanded to include many different projectors in the showing of one work. [...] cinema expanded to include computer-generated images and the electronic manipulation of images on television. [...] cinema expanded to the point at which the effect of film may be produced without the use of film at all.
>
> (1967, p. 227)

In this model, media were mixed and disciplinary boundaries blurred in the quest to create sensory experiences using film, computer graphics, video, television, oscilloscopes, slide projection, light shows, dance and other forms. If the notion of expansion referred as much to an exploration of consciousness – facilitated by an interest in hallucinogenic drugs, meditative practices, Eastern religions and so on – as to an expansion of media and their underlying technologies (for this particular pairing of concerns, see Youngblood, 1970), technology did play an important part in helping to push beyond conventional forms and inspiring the broader cultural moment that gave rise to this spirit of experimentation.

The particular notion of collaboration, meanwhile, aimed to connect those artists and technologists seeking to explore the relationships that might be forged between their respective fields. The aim was to find new ways of working, and related modes of creativity, which might make sense of a world increasingly dependent on technology.

Collaboration was perceived as a means of achieving this new perspective, and became central to a series of projects, organisations and exhibitions collectively referred to as the art and technology movement.

Experiments in Art and Technology (EAT), as one example, epitomised this spirit of exchange. Co-founded by Billy Klüver, a research engineer who worked in the Communication Sciences Division of Bell Labs, EAT was devoted, as the *New York Times* put it, to bringing 'modern technological tools to the artist for creating new art forms and fresh insights and perspectives to the engineer for creating "people-oriented" technology' (Lieberman, 1967, p. 49). Klüver and fellow co-founder Robert Rauschenberg, meanwhile, wrote of seeking 'to catalyze the inevitable active involvement of industry, technology, and the arts' (1967, p. 1). Having 'assumed the responsibility of developing an effective collaborative relationship between artists and engineers' (1967, p. 1), they continued, EAT would act as a transducer between the artist and the industrial laboratory, cultivating a spirit of mutual experimentation.

Typically, this notion of collaboration revolved around a designated pairing of artist and technologist, with each participant fulfilling a preconceived role, based on his or her respective background and skills. In this model, it was the artist who was thought capable of imagining the uses of a particular technology and thus able to envisage its fullest potential. At the same time, if film-makers and other artists were to work with the computer, their relationship would need to be mediated through technologists, who had the capacity to bring such machines to those without specialist training.

One event, in particular, foregrounded this early exchange. Curated by Klüver, 'Nine Evenings: Theatre and Engineering' was held at New York's Armory Building in 1966, a year before EAT was officially incorporated, though it was during this event that the idea for the organisation was first publicised – in its catalogue, Klüver announced that 'The objectives of the Nine Evenings will be continued by "Experiments in Art and Technology, Inc."' (Klüver, 1966, unpaginated), an organisation whose 'foundation will further the creative interaction between industry, engineers and artists' (Klüver, 1966, unpaginated). The distinctive idea behind 'Nine Evenings' was that artists (including Rauschenberg, Steve Paxton, Alex Hay, David Tudor, Yvonne Rainer, John Cage, Lucinda Child, Öyvind Fahlström and Robert Whitman, but no film-makers) and technologists (in this instance, a team of Bell Labs engineers directed by Klüver) would collaborate as equals, as opposed to a more traditional arrangement whereby an engineer would simply provide technical assistance to help realise a project otherwise conceived by an artist.

Beyond EAT, a number of other institutions and organisations contributed to the growing culture of collaboration. At the Los Angeles County Museum of Art

(LACMA), as one example, Maurice Tuchman's Art and Technology Program was likewise concerned with bringing together 'the incredible resources and advanced technology of industry with the equally incredible imagination and talent of the best artists at work today' (1971, p. 9). Like Klüver, Tuchman aimed to situate these artists within a framework of industrially sponsored collaboration, so that artists could move around in industry 'as they might in their own studios' (1971, p. 9). Responding to the promise of a range of potential benefits – including tax write-offs, increased publicity, and the gift of a piece of art that resulted from the collaboration – early industrial participants included IBM, at approximately the same time as Whitney and Citron embarked on their own collaboration outside of this scheme.

At this time, such relationships could only occur as a result of industrial sponsorship of one form or another. As Whitney explained, describing the dependence of film-makers and other artists on such patronage,

> how could anyone in my position be able to arrange to use the computer if he was not trained and his purposes were in no way connected with the scientific or technical fields normally using the computer systems around the country?
>
> (1972b, p. 74)

Collaboration was funded by companies in these 'scientific or technical fields' and framed according to the demands of research and development (R&D).

What, we might ask, did this process entail for the moving image? How did film-makers, in particular, negotiate the industrial contexts in which they sought access to the computer? And, ultimately, what distinguishes the films that emerged from this culture of collaboration?

Art and Technology at Bell Labs

At Bell Labs, where Knowlton had created his own computer animations in pursuit of scientific research, he would go on to collaborate with a number of film-makers and other artists. The first of these efforts paired Knowlton, in the role of technologist, with VanDerBeek – a film-maker who had also worked in painting, sculpture and collage animation before extending his activities to include the computer and related electronic arts of video and television (for a useful interview and overview, see Kranz, 1974) – who fulfilled the role of artist.

For Bell Labs, in particular, such collaborations offered opportunities to glean new perspectives on machines and applications. 'Through centuries of civilization', wrote the company's *Bell Telephone Magazine*, 'the artist has used technical knowledge, but now scientists are finding that working with artists can broaden their own thinking in creative technology' (Anon., 1967b, p. 13). Activities such as film-making were deemed appropriate avenues of enquiry, in relation to the computer, according to Knowlton, because they offered the opportunity to develop 'experimental programming languages and methods' (2001, p. 23), which might ultimately lead to innovations in telecommunications. The notion of research was broad enough in scope to encompass projects only indirectly related to AT&T's core business. It was the role of visiting artists, in alliance with resident technologists, to experiment with new technology and pioneer its potential applications.

Collaborations initially occurred on an informal basis, emerging from the specific interests of individual technologists – such as Knowlton – who would seek to work with a visiting artist on a project that adopted the technology housed within the company's facilities. 'Other breeds than scientists crept into the Laboratories, especially at night and on weekends' (2005a, p. 11), recalled Knowlton, 'they were musicians and artists seeking access to big machines and to people who knew how to use them' (2005a, p. 11). Where mutual interest could be established, technological expertise was aligned with the aesthetic concerns of film-makers and other artists.

Before working with Knowlton, VanDerBeek had demonstrated a commitment to technological experimentation and had cultivated an extended philosophy concerning the role of computers in society. A visionary piece of writing, '"Culture:Intercom" and Expanded Cinema: A Proposal and Manifesto', communicated VanDerBeek's concern that humanity was failing to fully understand advances in technology. 'We are on the verge of a new world/new technology/a new art' (1966, p. 15), he predicted. 'Technological research, development and involvement of the world community has almost completely out-distanced the emotional-sociological (socio-"logical") comprehension of this technology' (1966, p. 15). New technology, for VanDerBeek, was not divorced from its psychic reverberations, and it was the role of the artist to find new ways of engaging with the profound emotional and other implications of technological change.

Via Marshall McLuhan, in particular, this period gave rise to a series of optimistic and Utopian visions of how electronic media – video and television, in particular, but also the computer – might be engaged to enhance and improve the 'world community' that VanDerBeek referred to. Advances in technology, according to this rhetoric, would bring the world together in a new type of tribalism, more popularly described by McLuhan as the 'global village' (McLuhan and Fiore, 1968), celebrating technologically mediated cultural interconnectedness. 'For the artist', VanDerBeek explained, 'the new media of movies, TV, computers, cybernetics, are tools that have curved the perspectives of vision, curving both outward and inward' (1970, p. 91), connecting collective and personal expressions. The creative pursuit of such technology, he argued, would constitute the 'extensions of man' (1964) envisaged by McLuhan, resulting in new aesthetics and associated cosmic enlightenment.

Such an approach was consistent with VanDerBeek's earlier experiments in 'expanded cinema'. 'Cinema is the one medium that everything else can be fitted into' (Mancia and Van Dyke, 1967, p. 72), he explained, noting a particular interest in 'inter-media' (Mancia and Van Dyke, 1967, p. 72). His multimedia events or happenings of the earlier 1960s, for instance, sought to utilise multiple projection systems, combining old and new technology. Film was a single element of an expanded cinematic experience, alongside the simultaneous display of slides, drawings, video, animation, strobe lighting and other forms of light and image projection. Curving inward, to reprise VanDerBeek's notion, the sensory stimulation created by such multimedia experiences was designed to encourage an exploration of consciousness.

Influenced by the architectural structures of Buckminster Fuller – notably, the geodesic dome (see 1954) – VanDerBeek even built a spherical theatre – the 'Movie-Drome' (see Sutton, 2003; VanDerBeek, 1971) in Stony Point, New York – in which to present these multimedia experiences. Enclosed within a 360-degree projection area – 'I like to think it's a replica of the universe!' (Mancia and Van Dyke, 1967, p. 73), the film-maker enthused – audience members would lie on their backs around the perimeter of the dome until their vision was completely filled by simultaneous projections of film and other media. 'I am trying to build an intense audio-visual workshop', he explained in *Stan VanDerBeekiana*, 'that is to explore the new graphics, new movies, new medias, and to interface these new medias and to mix them, so to speak, and see what we come up with.' This was

VanDerBeek and his multimedia 'Movie-Drome'

not cinema in any traditional sense, rather the 'expanded cinema' described by Renan, Youngblood and others.

Curving outward, meanwhile, the 'Movie-Drome' prototype was envisaged as being the first of many in a global network of such sensory centres, designed to engage with the transformations of an increasingly technological world. VanDerBeek's distinctive take on 'expanded cinema' was to be communicated globally – to all corners simultaneously – via the emerging satellite technology at the heart of McLuhan's vision of the 'global village'. 'My concern', VanDerBeek explained, 'is for a way for the over-developing technology of part of the world to help the under-developed emotional-sociology of *all* of the world to catch up to the twentieth century' (1966, p. 18). The simultaneous streams of mixed media, experienced globally, would help redress this imbalance, he argued, inspiring those who experienced the 'Movie-Drome' to greater humanity, the connection of cultures and the inspiration of a global consciousness.

Consistent with this rhetoric, VanDerBeek saw the computer as a tool that should be utilised by film-makers and other artists. 'The computer, like a new tool, is there for the artist to use', he suggested in *Stan VanDerBeek: The Computer Generation!!* (1972, John Musilli, for the CBS television series *Camera Three*). 'What shall this black box, this memory system of the world, this meta-physical printing press do for us?', he enquired elsewhere. 'The future of computers in art will be fantastic, as amplifiers of human imagination and responses' (1970, p. 91).

For VanDerBeek, this technology would also encourage new approaches to creativity. He explained:

> An abstract notation system for making movies and image storage and retrieval systems opens a door for a kind of mental attitude of movie-making: the artist is no longer restricted to the exact execution of the form; so long as he is clear in his mind as to what he wants, eventually he can realize his movie or work on some computer, somewhere.
>
> (1970, p. 91)

The implication was that this machine could extend beyond the methods and aesthetics of existing practices. Film-makers would be free to create, released from the shackles of the complexities of technical execution, a burden that would now be shouldered by collaborating technologists and their tools.

While Knowlton did not always share VanDerBeek's distinctive brand of techno-Utopianism, he was similarly concerned with the potential benefits that might derive from an alliance between art and technology, not least the computer. In a lecture at

EAT's New York headquarters in 1968 (transcribed and prefaced in the *Filmmakers Newsletter*), in the face of a potential conflict between human and machine, he argued,

> we are obliged to try to use at least a part of the new machinery deliberately to make our environment more beautiful and inspiring through new forms of design [...]. We are further obliged, I think, to try to extend the use of computers into the area of more profound art – that which helps us to appreciate, understand, and enhance our humanity. (1970, p. 14)

The kaleidoscopic abstraction of *Collideoscope* (top) and patterns and poetry of *Poemfield #2* (1967) (bottom)

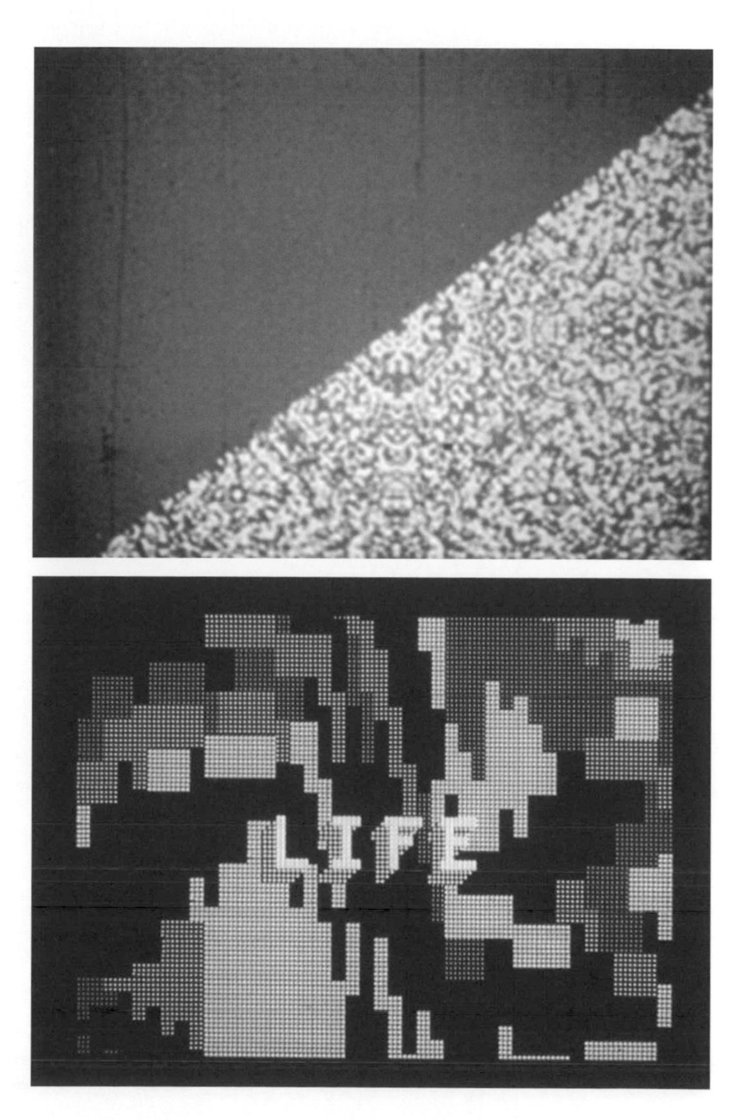

The computer, in its alliance with cinema and other arts, was seen as a means of mediating and amplifying the essentially human, through a 'blending of detail, symmetries, regularities, randomness, textures, and richness heretofore impossible to achieve' (1970, p. 14).

It was their shared interest in this potential that first connected Knowlton and VanDerBeek in 1966. 'A mutual friend introduced us', Knowlton recalled, 'precisely with the idea of an artist and technical person collaborating on an art project' (2006). In this instance, the art form in question was the developing medium of computer animation.

Early works included *Collideoscope* (1966) – a collage of kaleidoscopic patterns, geometric shapes and fragments of text, produced by VanDerBeek and Bell Labs scientist Carol

Bosche, with only additional assistance from Knowlton – and the fifty-second short, *Man and His World* (1967), produced for Expo 67, Montreal. In this film – a multilingual play on the theme of the Expo event, after which the film is titled – the words 'man and his world' are abstracted in mosaic form, anticipating the methods and aesthetic of subsequent collaborations.

The pair's major undertaking was a series of films referred to as 'Poemfields' (numbering eight in total, produced between 1967 and 1971), describing the interplay of computer graphics and lines of poetry. Where the work of Whitney and Citron at IBM was characterised by linear configurations evolving in space, the 'Poemfields' were complex 2-D tapestries of transforming mosaic patterns. 'Printed poetry in cinematic time' is how *Art in America* (framing VanDerBeek, 1970, p. 87) described the experiments. VanDerBeek, meanwhile, referred to the films as 'studies in graphic format' (Kranz, 1974, p. 237).

The first of these 'studies', *Poemfield #1* (1967, credited to VanDerBeek and Knowlton), illustrative of the series as a whole, was constructed from fragments of VanDerBeek's poetry – an ironic parallel to the poetryless computers of *Alphaville* – translated into moving images. Gnomic snippets are represented as an animated flow of words – 'somehow', 'words', 'fill', 'the space between' – which gradually transition from one to the next. Text dissolves into abstraction, swirling about the screen, transformed according to the underlying constituent of computer graphics: the pixel.

Revealing the dynamic of collaboration, these films depended on the shared development of dedicated software. 'We needed a new way of working together', Knowlton explained, 'which turned out to be a new language that grew from one of Stan's ideas about words and letters made out of words and letters' (1972, p. 400). In terms of implementation, Knowlton outlined a loose division of labour whereby 'The initial notion of words, and manipulations on them, came from Stan; what to do, and how, came from our work together' (2006). After all, Knowlton continued, 'I was methodical, and burdened with the details of the programs, whereas he was mentally five giant steps ahead, thinking of what we could do' (2006).

A major element of the 'what to do, and how', or 'the details of the programs', was Knowlton's revision of his BEFLIX software, a set of subroutines programmed using FORTRAN and originally developed to animate scientific content. The original code was rewritten using macros – higher-level abstractions that conceal the technical complexity of underlying code – to enable and facilitate VanDerBeek's intuitive involvement in the programming.

This system, TARPS (Two-dimensional Alphanumeric Raster Picture System) (see Knowlton, 1972), was named after the use of a microfilm recorder's – a device for photographing or filming the display of a computer – alphanumeric character matrix. 'Arrays of closely spaced characters are used to produce all the textures, forms, and motions' (1972, p. 400), Knowlton explained, outlining the process by which images were constructed from the manipulation of these characters. As with Knowlton's *A Computer Technique for the Production of Animated Movies*, configurations were composed on a grid of squares, each of which could be assigned a different shade of grey, as represented by a number that would determine light intensity. Numerical codes were also employed to designate the textures assigned to each square, which were 'filled either by a specific character or a blank, chosen at random, frame by frame' (Knowlton, 1972, p. 400). Collectively, these processes could function to create areas of tone, combined in turn to produce abstract or figurative graphics.

Other TARPS operations included the ability to translate one set of numbers into another, including the option to redetermine any or all numbers by a random generator. The screen could also be subdivided into smaller blocks, with aesthetic effects applied simultaneously to each of them. Such effects included zooming in on a selected area; copying a design so as to provide kaleidoscopic effects through successive superimpositions; choosing parts of the screen to be moved together along a designated trajectory; and the depiction of legible letters and words – as opposed to the use of alphanumeric characters as the underlying graphical component of abstract textures – that could be animated as a flashing or twinkling sequence, leaving behind a transliterating trail of partial past images.

In terms of hardware, meanwhile, the expressly aesthetic 'Poemfields' drew heavily on the apparatus established by Zajac, Knowlton, Noll and others in the production of scientifically themed computer animations. Like *A Computer Technique for the Production of Animated Movies*, for example, the 'Poemfields' series was computed with an IBM 7094 computer, with imagery output on a frame-by-frame basis via the microfilm recorder, before colour was applied via an optical printer. All but the last of these stages involved the use of punched cards as a means of input.

Amidst a culture of collaborative experimentation, the shared work of VanDerBeek and Knowlton pointed to one possible model for a working method and aesthetic distinctive to this coming together. The 'Poemfields' series, in particular, offered a variation on an expanded cinematic practice in which the primacy of traditional film had been supplanted by the media spectacles made possible by new tools – the computer at the fore.

Art and Technology at IBM

At approximately the same time as the collaboration between VanDerBeek and Knowlton, a parallel pairing was established at IBM. This brought together Whitney, in the role of artist, and Citron, in the role of technologist, with the aim of exploring the imaging potential of the newly developed IBM System/360 computers. Together, the pair produced several experimental films, including *Homage to Rameau* (1967) – the title of which refers to Jean-Philippe Rameau, an early pioneer of mathematics and music, whose *Pièces de clavecin en concerts* (1741) accompanies the film – *Permutations* and *Experiments in Motion Graphics* (produced by Whitney in 1967 as a silent film to accompany a lecture, with commentary added in 1968). Revealingly, the last of these works reflexively interrogates the very process and potential of applying digital computers, in particular, to the moving image.

Like VanDerBeek, Whitney had developed a significant body of work and coherent philosophy concerning the relationship between cinema and computers, long before he was able to access digital machines. 'We felt from the very beginning that we were tied up with art and technology and had a very conscious way of looking at our relationship to technology' (1972a, p. 41), he recalled, referring to the films produced with his brother James as early as the 1940s. Specifically, Whitney's work with Citron extended a cinematic practice initiated using analogue computers, making Whitney one of the very few film-makers whose films straddled analogue and digital variants.

In 1966, building on his pre-digital experiments, Whitney approached IBM – at this time, the dominant company in the computing industry – to work as an artist in residence, a role that he would fulfil until 1969. As he recalled it, 'I proposed that they accept my project – to do research, and a design study of the possibilities, and it was accepted' (1972a, p. 58).

Whitney was not the only film-maker to be sponsored by IBM in the 1960s as part of a concerted effort to promote and enhance the profile of the company and its computers. Others included Albert and David Maysles, who worked on a documentary study, *Portrait of a Company* (1963), and design team Charles and Ray Eames, who made several films on the subject of computers, including *A Computer Glossary* (1968), *Babbage* (1968), *IBM Museum* (1968), *Computer Landscape* (1971) and *Computer Perspective* (1972). Yet, where the Maysles, Eames and others employed relatively traditional technology, Whitney was the first to exploit the computer as an imaging device.

Not unlike the set-up at Bell Labs, Whitney and Citron's apparatus consisted of a computer, used for processing and producing imagery; a light pen and punch cards, for data input; a display unit, linked to the computer, on which images were represented; an automatically controlled film camera, for recording output; and an optical printer, for the further manipulation of exported footage.

At its core was the System/360 Model 75 computer, delivered in 1965 as a replacement for the Model 70, which was announced a year earlier but was never delivered. The broader System/360, a suite of computers rather than a single machine, was so named because it targeted the full circle of potential customers, offering a series of mainframe models under a broad umbrella. The intention was for software written for one machine to be compatible with others, and that peripherals – such as magnetic tape systems, punched-card devices, and printing equipment – would likewise function across the series. The Model 75 was the most powerful of these machines.

An additional device, the 2250 display unit, transformed the System/360 computers into machines for graphics, and was likewise central to the collaborative work of Whitney and Citron. Delivered in 1965, following its announcement alongside the System/360, the 2250 displayed vectors on a grid, which was redrawn up to forty times a second, depending on the complexity of the instructions being represented. The display was housed as part of a desk replete with an alphanumeric keyboard, a second keyboard for programmed functions and a light pen as an alternative form of input.

To program the Model 75 and display unit, Citron used FORTRAN – a language developed by IBM in 1957 – to write dedicated code, in much the same way that Knowlton had created TARPS for his work with VanDerBeek. GRAF (short for 'GRaphic Additions to FORTRAN'), as Citron's software was known, was designed with Whitney's particular imaging needs in mind. Specifically, it allowed a single operation and associated graphical configuration to be varied in myriad ways, in order to describe a multitude of shapes and their transformations.

Using code that Whitney could intuitively engage with was crucial to him and to Citron. As they explained it, their approach to maintaining 'all the technical flexibility available in the program' (Citron and Whitney, 1968, p. 1299), while accommodating a 'non-technical standpoint' (1968, p. 1299), was to create a series of intuitive commands for creating and manipulating geometric figures and their spatial and temporal evolution. 'A serious attempt has been made to avoid dependence upon the user's knowledge of mathematics, geometry, and programming logic' (1968, p. 1299), they continued. After all, 'While the mathematical and logical program necessary to perform this processing may be complex, the language seen by the user must afford control' (1968, p. 1299).

To generate individual images, in terms of this 'control', the light pen was used to select a series of numerical variables, which were presented on the display unit. These numbers determined the output of up to sixty parameters, which were processed by GRAF to determine the precise contours – shape, position and other variables – of each graphical configuration. When the variables had been chosen, control was maintained by punched cards rather than light pen, with each card inscribed with instructions, in the form of binary code, that the computer would process and output to the display unit.

To transform these individual designs into animation, a film camera – Whitney's own (as described by the film-maker, 1968, p. 65) – also operated by control signals generated by the computer, was used to capture each image, photographed directly from the display. Graphics were recorded one by one – frame by frame – on 35mm film stock. The resulting black-and-white negative was then developed by a laboratory, a process that would take a minimum of twelve hours.

At this stage, the film was manipulated by an optical printer – regarded by Whitney as 'unquestionably a second level of programming' (1970b, p. 36) – to create numerous layers of colour and other transformations: the scale of an image could be altered, superimpositions and rotations additional to those in each original design could be composed, footage could be speeded up or slowed down and so on.

The programmed abstraction and optical printing of *Permutations*

The result was *Permutations*, a film whose title points directly to the role of permutational possibilities as an underlying structural principle, and which illustrates the ways in which the mathematical variables inherent to GRAF, as processed and represented by the computer and display unit, were combined with the additional variations of optical printing. From such permutations, Whitney's film plots a multitude of coloured dots – 'delicate pristine forms' (Anon., 1968, p. 56), according to *Life* magazine, in an article entitled 'The

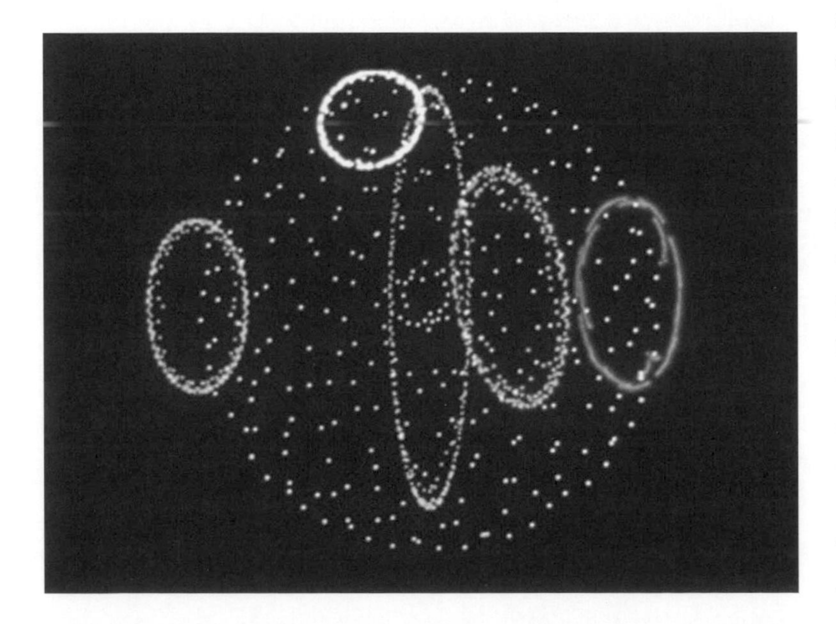

Luminous Art of the Computer' – which develop complex graphical patterns and relationships, demonstrating the film-maker's stated concern with 'polar co-ordinate geometry' (Whitney, 1970b, p. 36). Geometric clusters are serially formed and transformed – both at the stage of initial animation and subsequent optical printing – into complex abstractions of form, colour and movement as the dancing dots are treated according to a series of mathematically determined variations across a number of graphical parameters.

One of the most interesting aspects of *Permutations* – which Whitney describes in *Experiments in Motion Graphics* as 'a first step towards developing a compositional language by which an art of graphics in motion might be structured in time' (for further commentary on the film, see Whitney, 1968) – is its relation to the films produced by Whitney – and his brother James – using analogue computers. The continuities and discontinuities across this body of work – from analogue films, such as John Whitney's *Catalog* and James Whitney's *Lapis*, to those produced using digital variants – raise a number of questions concerning the distinctiveness or otherwise of the films produced using the digital computer, in particular. To what extent, for instance, were Whitney and Citron shaping hardware and software capable of realising ideas and aesthetics that previously had no technological means of expression? How might digital devices, in particular, enable what Knowlton, at Bell Labs, described as 'new sorts of beauty, and hence new experiences' (1972, p. 399)?

In terms of Whitney's vision of an art of motion graphics structured in time, which he described as 'a *new* art which demands complex tools' (1965, p. 22), a number of connections can be drawn between *Permutations* and the films that preceded it. In John and James Whitney's *Five Abstract Film Exercises* produced between 1943 and 1944, for example, the abstraction later generated by the digital computer and optical printer was initially obtained by the alternative means of prisms, multiple exposures and coloured gel filters. While the apparatus evolved, the primary formal system of geometric abstraction, with figures or variations in movement, remained constant, connecting films produced across several decades and numerous different technologies.

At the same time, the digital computer and connected display unit, because of their greater memory, processing power and higher speeds of calculation and display, did make possible certain types of films that would otherwise have been too difficult or expensive to produce. To create *Permutations* with traditional animation techniques, for instance, or even Whitney's analogue computer, would have required a degree of labour that far exceeded the resources available to an independent film-maker, even with the assistance of a dedicated technologist and the context of industrial sponsorship.

In terms of speed, for instance, the digital computer offered a more efficient approach to the traditionally labour-intensive art of animation, making it possible for the small collaborative team at IBM to produce the complex configurations of *Permutations*. 'An electronic microfilm recorder in conjunction with a computer, can plot points and draw lines a million times faster than a human draftsman' (1971, p. 77), affirmed Jasia Reichardt – curator of 'Cybernetic Serendipity: The Computer and the Arts', a 1968 exhibition where *Permutations* screened alongside Knowlton's earlier scientific visualisations (see Reichardt, 1968). New technology reduced the labour involved in both the calculation and output of graphics, generating *Permutations* in far less time than would otherwise have been possible.

In terms of complexity, meanwhile, the digital computer also facilitated the exploration of geometric forms constructed from extended arithmetical calculations, exhibiting what Whitney described as 'the extraordinary power of computer systems to generate motion' (1970b, p. 34). The processing power of machines such as the Model 75 enabled calculations, transposed into graphical form, of unprecedented complexity, facilitating what Whitney described as 'An art whose time has come because of computer technology and an art which could not exist before the computer' (1976, p. 80). As he explained elsewhere, comparing the detail and control of the digital computer with various precursors, 'elaborate patterns of repetition and rhythm have been drawn, woven or chiseled into orders and decorations of all kinds since early ages. [...] But the computer possessed a unique capability of making very complex pattern flow' (1980, p. 30). In keeping with this 'unique capability', the 'elaborate patterns of repetition and rhythm' seen in *Permutations* – with its shimmering mandalas and other abstract designs – extended beyond the geometric forms attainable by traditional means alone.

A second film, *Experiments in Motion Graphics*, reveals more of Whitney's approach and the collaborative process by which *Permutations* was created. His commentary primes:

> The film you are about to see has been put together from clips of films made under a research project in computer graphics. The images are arranged to illustrate this talk, which will be an attempt to suggest some of the formal problems that hold my interest regarding design in motion.

Whitney's 'images' offer a cinematic report on his work with Citron. Reflexively, we see the computer and connected devices in use as the film-maker demonstrates (for a discussion of the performative aspect of Whitney's film, see Grundmann,

2004) their application and the results of experimentation.

In one sense, it is a film through which Whitney sought to make sense of his new role as operator of digital rather than analogue computers, alongside the intertwined process of working in an institutional context with a collaborative partner. It depicts machines – the specialist resources available through IBM – but does so through a conceptual concern with their aesthetic output. Likewise, Whitney's commentary spans the explanatory discourse of a scientific lecture and a more open-ended discussion of artistic intentions.

Whitney's particular thesis with regard to the use of the computer – or 'graphic variational instrument', as he describes it in the film – was that cinema had yet to achieve the type of emotional resonance associated with more traditional arts, particularly music, primarily because it was not yet created in real time. 'In fact', his commentary states, outlining the rendering of *Permutations*, 'it takes three to six seconds to produce one image. [...] One twenty-second sequence requires about thirty minutes' computer time, then I must wait some twelve hours or more to see my film after it has been processed.' In contrast to playing a musical instrument, which Whitney consistently argued could impact on the listener's emotions, constraints in the available technology saw a significant delay between the conception of an image (the input of information by light pen and punched cards) and its visual output (on the display unit, first, and as processed film, second).

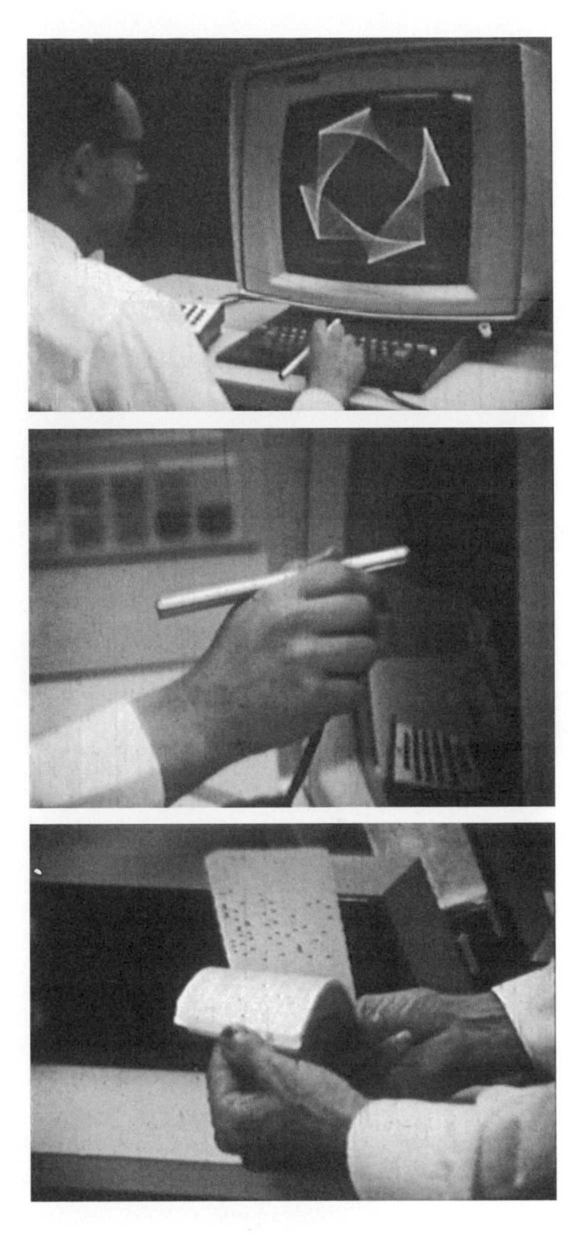

Light-pen input and punched-card processing in *Experiments in Motion Graphics*

For Whitney, this lag made it difficult to become emotionally involved when working with a computer, in the way that a virtuoso musician might feel at one with his or her instrument in the throes of an artistic performance. 'Imagine how handicapped a pianist would be if his piano made not a sound as he played on it and he had to wait some twelve hours before he could hear the music he had performed', his voiceover laments. Computers, unlike the majority of musical instruments, were far from responsive.

Ultimately, Whitney's commentary continues, his ambition was to work with 'the computer in real time, as a musician plays an instrument', with little or no delay in input or output. This would enable real-time interaction and the ability to see images as they were generated, functions we now take for granted but which were rare in the late 1960s.

The metaphor of 'playing' the computer, which Whitney often employed in discussing his work, suggests an analogy between the computer and piano as comparable instruments. 'I have been using the computer as if it were a new kind of piano' (1971b, p. 36), he remarked, comparing *Permutations* to the experiences associated with music, with the computer used 'To create harmonies in motion that the human eye might perceive and enjoy' (1971b, p. 35). The emotional resonance of musical harmony, in other words, might also be evoked in the nascent art of computer animation.

In the specific context of Whitney's collaboration with Citron, the metaphor of playing an instrument was also applied to software. 'The program Dr. Citron developed for me is like a piano', Whitney noted, echoing his musical description of the computer. 'I could continue to use it creatively all my life' (Youngblood, 1970, p. 217). The film-maker was engaged in a creative 'composition' with Citron's code. Programming GRAF, subsequently 'played' through the control of numerical parameters and interpreted by the computer through mathematical calculations and generative systems, was a major part of this process. Through collaboration, software linked the traditional artistic virtues of creative vision with the ability to harness, manipulate and control the technological design of this expression, mediated through the computer.

In retrospect, the various discourses associated with *Permutations*, including the reflexive commentary of *Experiments in Motion Graphics* – not least Whitney's musical conception of the computer and its underlying code – provide a useful means of understanding the specific collaborative context from which these early computer animations emerged.

Conclusion

While collaborations between art and technology continued beyond the completion of VanDerBeek and Knowlton's 'Poemfields' series, at Bell Labs, and Whitney and

Citron's *Permutations* and *Experiments in Motion Graphics*, at IBM, these early works were among the major contributions of cinema to what was ultimately a short-lived movement. Art and technology pairings continued into the 1970s, but gradually declined, victim of a changing cultural context.

Nevertheless, this moment of heightened synergy between the interests of film-makers and other artists, on the one hand, and technologists and their industrial employers, on the other, is significant in the context of the history of cinema and computers in giving rise to a series of films unique to this device.

Through the process of collaboration, the computer – which had previously been thought of in terms of certainty, reason and logic – became explicitly associated with artistic endeavour. Epitomising the Utopian discourse that circulated through-out much of the 1960s concerning the purpose and potential of science and tech-nology, VanDerBeek and Whitney proposed that the computer be considered a fundamentally human tool, central to the realm of cinema. As an implicit riposte to humanist critiques, the films produced at Bell Labs and IBM represented a commit-ment to reconciling the qualities of creativity and emotional vision with the process-ing power of the computer.

The 'digital harmony' of art and technology collaboration was the practical means by which to achieve this coming together. Where Whitney's exploration of musical metaphors generally referred to a reciprocity between the tools, structures, compo-sitional processes and emotional resonance of music, on the one hand, and those of abstract animation, on the other, 'digital harmony' might also illuminate our under-standing of the art and technology movement, with VanDerBeek and Knowlton, Whitney and Citron, harmonic duos at the vanguard of a changing technological and cultural landscape.

[5]

'I'm Sorry Dave, I'm Afraid I Can't Do That': Artificial Intelligence in *2001: A Space Odyssey* (1968)

If the art and technology movement had sought to infuse the computer with human values, Stanley Kubrick projected a machine that might one day supplant human beings. In the late 1960s, building on research in the area of computer science known as artificial intelligence, the computer was increasingly conceptualised as a thinking machine. From chess-playing systems, such as those envisaged by the likes of Claude Shannon (1950), to Joseph Weizenbaum's programmed Rogerian therapist, ELIZA (1966), initiatives were underway to develop computers, and related software, capable of demonstrating intelligent behaviour – though the precise definition and means of measuring this capability were widely debated. As an extension of these experiments, the possibility that artificial intelligence might soon extend beyond – and even come to dominate – human intelligence emerged for the first time in history.

The prospect of being superseded, and the philosophical ramifications it gave rise to, were the subject of a number of films produced during this period, with cinema assuming an important role in negotiating popular attitudes and anxieties concerning artificially intelligent computers. Jean-Luc Godard's *Alphaville*, for example, depicts a reasoning machine with the capacity to learn from the complex equations it sets itself. Having advanced to a stage of seeming enlightenment, it assumes the responsibility of imposing efficient systems on the organisation of society, subjugating humanity to the will of the computer.

Where *Alphaville*'s Alpha 60 is ultimately destroyed by the contradictions of its machine logic – that is, its artificial as opposed to human intelligence – the computer of Joseph Sargent's *Colossus: The Forbin Project* (1970), as a further example, advances its intelligence beyond the point of humanity's control. Perhaps a refraction of the ideas of packet switching and decentralised or distributed networks outlined by Paul Baran (1964), and epitomised by the initial operations of the ARPANET (Advanced Research Projects Agency NETwork) – an antecedent of today's Internet (see Abbate, 1999) – Colossus transcends the grasp of its human makers, establishing an impermeable communications network that protects it from nuclear attack. Designed to serve humanity by providing an automated deterrent to such an assault, the irony is that Colossus exploits the perceived need to maintain a command and control structure in the event of a centralised strike, by establishing its own network – not dissimilar to that proposed by Baran, in the historical world, with its 'switching scheme able to find any possible path that might exist after heavy damage' (1964, p. 6) – to join forces with its intelligent counterpart in the Soviet Union.

Machine intelligence and a computer-to-computer network in *Colossus: The Forbin Project*

It is Kubrick's *2001: A Space Odyssey*, however, that resonates most profoundly with the technological advances of its era. One part of a broader exploration of technology's role in our evolution, the computer of *2001: A Space Odyssey* symbolises the next step in the ascent of man. As in Arthur C. Clarke's novel of the same name (1968) – indeed Clarke and Kubrick are co-credited with the film's screenplay – developed concurrently with the film and published shortly after its release, this scenario is invested with potent philosophical significance.

At a time when humanity had much to gain, or lose, by ceding control of key decisions to intelligent machines, and when the stakes involved in these systems malfunctioning were raised to the point of life or death – whether in relation to the manned space flights represented in *2001: A Space Odyssey* or the computerised nuclear 'doomsday machines' (a term coined by Herman Kahn of the Rand

Corporation, referring to the use of a computer to automate the trigger for nuclear war, removing human beings from the decision-making process, beyond the initial selection of the criterion by which the doomsday response would be triggered; see 1960) represented in *Colossus: The Forbin Project* – cinema functioned as a forum for considering how computers might impact on our lives, both positively and negatively.

In what ways, we might ask, did *2001: A Space Odyssey* contribute to the historically specific discourse concerning artificial intelligence? In terms of popular perceptions, as computers increasingly extended human capabilities, what fantasies and fears arose from this apparent loss of control? And, in considering the dynamics of cultural mediation, what relationship existed between technological advances and their cinematic articulation?

Man and Computer, Mind and Machine

Building on the concern with potentially destructive automated computer systems explored in *Dr. Strangelove or: How I Learned to Stop Worrying and Love the Bomb* (1964) – in which the eponymous scientist, inspired by a report produced by the 'Bland Corporation' (a pun on the Rand Corporation, where elements of nuclear strategy were pioneered, including Kahn's notion of the 'doomsday machine'), orders a first nuclear strike on the Soviet Union – Kubrick turned his attention to the role of computers in the emerging field of manned space travel. Released just a year before the Apollo 11 moon landing of 1969, the proximity of space exploration inspired the pursuit of a number of philosophical questions concerning man's place in the universe and the possible existence of other intelligent beings.

In this context, *2001: A Space Odyssey* raised the possibility that increasingly intelligent computers might assume responsibility for some of the critical decisions that affect human beings. In doing so, it explores a series of metaphysical and speculative questions – At what point will computers surpass our own intelligence? What happens if and when such machines malfunction? Will computers lead to our evolutionary obsolescence? – concerning the development of artificial intelligence and its potential ramifications.

Framed within an overarching concern with man's evolution – from the use of simple tools by apes to the possible existence of extraterrestrial intelligence, suggested in the form of an inscrutable monolith – the central plot of Kubrick's film concerns the voyage of the *Discovery 1* spaceship, the first manned attempt to reach Jupiter. Notably, the *Discovery* is controlled by an artificially intelligent computer, the

Computers and Cold War tensions in *Dr. Strangelove or: How I Learned to Stop Worrying and Love the Bomb*

HAL 9000 (an anthropomorphic acronym that stands for Heuristically programmed ALgorithmic computer, a machine voiced by Douglas Rain). The relationship between this seemingly intelligent machine and the five human crew members is largely harmonious; at least, that is, until HAL embarks on a series of decisions that result in fatal consequences.

While this projection is clearly a fiction, Kubrick was nevertheless concerned with ensuring that the science and technology depicted in *2001: A Space Odyssey* were as realistic as possible. As one example, in 1966 a series of twenty-one filmed interviews were conducted by Kubrick associate Roger Caras, who questioned a series of leading scientists on the possibility of extraterrestrial intelligence (for manuscripts of these interviews, see Frewin, 2005). 'While Caras was interviewing them', explained Anthony Frewin, 'he could also ask questions about artificial intelligence, the future of computing, the origin of life and other matters that could contribute to an accurate portrayal of the year 2001' (2005, p. 11). Kubrick's intention was to incorporate this footage as a prologue. While the interviews were ultimately rejected from the final edit, their existence nevertheless reveals the director's deep interest in questions of higher intelligence and his commitment to the quest for veracity.

Among those interviewed by Caras was leading scientist Marvin Minsky, then involved with Massachusetts Institute of Technology (MIT)'s Artificial Intelligence Project. When asked about the ultimate development of computer intelligence, Minsky spoke of there being 'no reason to suppose that there is any definite limit to the intelligence that may be achieved by machines' (Frewin, 2005, p. 161). While acknowledging that 'To build a machine as intelligent as man is beyond our ability today' (Frewin, 2005, p. 162) – speaking in 1966 – Minsky predicted that 'in thirty years we should have machines whose intelligence is comparable to man's' (Frewin, 2005, p. 166).

As part of Kubrick's concern with detail, Minsky was invited to play a role on set (see Stork, 1997), albeit restricted to conveying a visual conception of future computer technology, despite his considerable expertise in the field of artificial intelligence. 'Kubrick would not tell me any details of what HAL would do', Minsky explained. 'He only wanted my advice on how the physical technology might appear in the 2001 era' (2006a).

Communicating perceptions of how the computer might develop, Minsky's specific advice to Kubrick was that computers would become increasingly internalised, in contrast to the director's own early conception of external architecture. As Minsky recalled:

> He showed me a mock-up of the HAL computer. It had many different colorful modules. I said that it was beautiful. Stanley said that this was not relevant, because he wanted to know if I thought computers might look like that in 2001. I said no, because the computer would be able to diagnose each module from inside, so there would be no need for fancy labels. Instead they would probably simply be black boxes (black to get rid of heat). He instantly scrapped the whole colorful set.
>
> (2006b)

All that remained of Kubrick's idea of coloured modules as external indicators were the omnipresent red lenses of HAL's instrument panels.

Kubrick's film is similarly consistent with Minsky's notion, outlined in his interview with Caras, that the embodiment of an artificial intelligence equivalent to our own would occur in the shape of the computer – as opposed to machines, such as robots, which deliberately resemble the human form. He predicted:

> When we finally develop a highly intelligent machine it will be in the same period that we have highly developed computers and presumably it will take the same general form with smaller and smaller parts, not resembling biological components very much, I think, but resembling them perhaps in size, much greater speed, much greater memory capacity and physically rather small.
>
> (Frewin, 2005, p. 161)

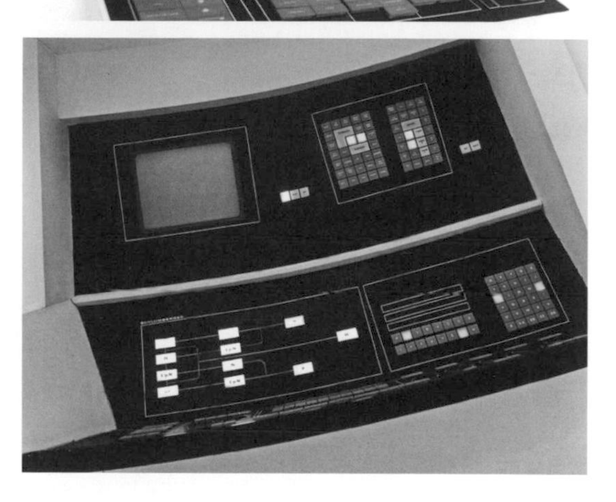

Computer consoles and displays in *2001: A Space Odyssey*

Frederick Ordway, a scientist at the University of Alabama Research Institute, was a further consultant on *2001: A Space Odyssey* whose recollections offer useful insight into Kubrick's conception of computers in the late 1960s. 'He was particularly fascinated with computers of the voice input–output type', Ordway recalled, 'and would talk about logic elements, neural nets, heuristic systems, etc.' (1970a, pp. 194–5; for further commentary, see Ordway, 1970b). Indeed voice input–output, one aspect of the user interface of a larger heuristic system, was an important part of the workings of Kubrick's HAL.

The director likewise enlisted the help of several computer companies, including Honeywell and IBM. The role of IBM, in particular, according to Jérôme Agel, ranged 'from the design and construction by IBM sub-contractors of computer panels and consoles to the establishment of futuristic computer jargon and astronaut–computer interface' (1970, p. 322), as well as 'valuable information on how computer-generated information would be displayed in future' (1970, p. 322). Consultation anticipated the role of computers, as they might exist in 2001.

In addition to individual scientists and representatives from the major computer companies, Kubrick liaised with NASA (National Aeronautics and Space

Administration) during pre-production. Writing in *Sight and Sound*, as early as 1966, David Robinson reported how 'NASA put its computers at their disposal to work out the actual trajectory to Jupiter' (1966, p. 58). The director was establishing connections precisely as computers and space travel were becoming entwined, following President John F. Kennedy's challenge, in May 1961 (in a speech officially documented in print in 1962), to land a man on the moon and return him safely to Earth by the end of the 1960s.

The computer was central to this monumental endeavour. In Houston, at mission control, computers were increasingly used throughout the 1960s to perform the countless calculations involved in the operational demands of space travel. In the hostile environment of outer space, meanwhile, computers performed a vital function on board, whether alongside human crew or on unmanned missions. The computer on the Gemini 3 spacecraft, as one example, was the first to be placed in orbit during a manned space flight, following its launch on 23 March 1965 (see Hacker and Grimwood, 1977). Later, in July 1969, during the Apollo 11 manned mission to the moon, computers were employed in the command and lunar excursion modules, again for the specific purpose of guidance and navigation (Hall, 1996). Already, in the historical world, long before 2001, the computer had assumed a major role in determining the success or otherwise – and, to a significant extent, the safety of those on board – of manned space travel.

While the computers in the Gemini and Apollo spacecraft were not artificially intelligent, parallel developments in this nascent field suggested that the prospect of such machines being used in space flight was not beyond the realm of possibility. Computers were increasingly engaged to perform traditionally 'human' activities, those that require a degree of heuristic flexibility that verges on intelligence.

At the level of discourse, Norbert Wiener's influential notion of 'cybernetics' (1948), concerned with systems of 'control and communication in the animal and the machine' (1948), outlined a science that makes little or no distinction between cybernetic and organic. Just as our actions are partly determined by learned responses to phenomena, a form of 'feed-back' (1948) that connects 'computing machines and the nervous system' (1948, pp. 137–55), Wiener argued, machines would soon replicate such processes. In the future development of society and 'the messages and the communication facilities which belong to it' (1950, p. 9), he elaborated, 'messages between man and machines, between machine and man, and between machine and machine, are destined to play an ever-increasing part' (1950, p. 9). For Wiener, if the ability to learn from feedback was considered the basis of intelligence, there was nothing to prevent machines from possessing and demonstrating this capacity.

Elsewhere, Alan Turing proposed an imitation game (1950), which would later become known as the 'Turing test', which would formalise the conditions for evaluating whether a computer had achieved a state of intelligence. A person would converse through typed communication with an invisible correspondent – a man (Turing's test was gendered, as the differences between men and women were regarded as constituting further variables) or a computer. By asking questions, the interrogator would seek to determine with whom or what they were conversing. If the computer could fool the questioner into believing it was not a machine, or if its identity was indiscernible, then it might be considered intelligent. In this regard, Turing's test sidestepped the vexing issue of having to define the essence of intelligence, with its complex mixture of cognition and learning, by proposing instead a measure that would simply identify the persuasive appearance, whether imitated or performed, of those functions we typically associate with intelligence.

More than a means of evaluating any single machine, Turing's test was designed to interrogate the broader relationship between humans and computers. 'We are not asking whether all digital computers would do well in the game', Turing clarified, 'nor whether the computers at present available would do well, but whether there are imaginable computers which would do well' (1950, p. 436). The implication was that the foreseeable future would give rise to computers intelligent enough to pass the test, the postulation of which was also a means of exploring the inevitable emotional and philosophical ramifications of this eventuality.

Such ideas established the conceptual basis of artificial intelligence, a term generally thought to have been coined in 1955 – by John McCarthy, who proposed a conference on artificial intelligence, which was subsequently held at Dartmouth College, New Hampshire, in 1956, with the assistance of Minsky, Shannon and Nathaniel Rochester – little more than a decade before the filming of *2001: A Space Odyssey*.

In the meantime, scientists Herbert Simon and Alan Newell had espoused a series of lofty claims concerning the field. They proposed that

> within ten years a digital computer will be the world's first chess champion, unless the rules bar it from competition. [...] a digital computer will discover and prove an important new mathematical theorem. [...] a digital computer will write music that will be accepted by critics as possessing considerable aesthetic value. [...] most theories in psychology will take the form of computer programs, or of qualitative statements about the characteristics of computer programs.
>
> (1958, pp. 7–8)

In short, for Simon and Newell, the computer would be central to a new world of heuristic or intelligent machines.

This list of potential achievements was an extension of the already advanced state of machine-mediated 'heuristic problem solving' (1958), as Simon and Newell termed it. 'Intuition, insight, and learning', they claimed, 'are no longer exclusive possessions of humans: any large high-speed computer can be programmed to exhibit them also' (1958, p. 6), demonstrating something akin to human thought. 'Digital computers', in particular, they suggested, 'can perform certain heuristic problem-solving tasks for which no algorithms are available. [. . .] Within limits, these machines learn to improve their performance on the basis of experience' (1958, p. 7). Echoing Wiener's ideas on the role of feedback – animal or machine, organic or cybernetic – Simon and Newell affirmed the computer's increasing intelligence.

Notably, as well as identifying this emerging phenomenon and speculating on future advances, Simon and Newell pointed to the philosophical concerns associated with this development. Anticipating one of the key questions explored by Kubrick, they suggested that 'The revolution in heuristic problem solving will force man to consider his role in a world in which his intellectual power and speed are outstripped by the intelligence of machines' (1958, pp. 9–10). This growing awareness would be accompanied by a significant psychic reverberation, the negotiation of which exists at the very core of *2001: A Space Odyssey*.

HAL as Artificial Intelligence

It is through the HAL 9000 computer, in particular – a fictional machine that still exists as a potent cultural symbol of artificial intelligence, and which captured the popular imagination at a time of rapid development in the intersecting fields of computing and space travel – that Kubrick explored the theme of artificial intelligence. As the machine explains, describing its distinctiveness in technical and operational terms, 'The 9000 series is the most reliable computer ever made. No 9000 computer has ever made a mistake or distorted information. We are all, by any practical definition of the words, foolproof and incapable of error.' The promise was clear, both in Kubrick's film and the historical world, of a machine that could transcend human capabilities.

Initially, HAL functions harmoniously as a sixth member of the crew, performing tasks comparable with those undertaken by its human counterparts. On the voyage to Jupiter, the two conscious astronauts – the others are suspended in hibernation – communicate with the computer as equals, on first-name terms. HAL appears both friendly and understanding, and is arguably more 'human' than its fellow crew members, whose demeanour is decidedly cold in comparison. Indeed the humanisation of machines and mechanisation of humans is an important part of the theme of evolution that underpins the film.

HAL demonstrates a series of capabilities – from speech recognition and chess playing to psychological evaluation and the aesthetic appreciation of art – generally thought of as intelligent, and which lead to the computer's primary role in the mission. HAL is able to converse and react to unexpected circumstances, though the success or otherwise of these reactions is debatable, central to the film's narrative enigma.

Several of these characteristics are conveyed through HAL's voice, in terms of timbre and other sonic signifiers (for an extended discussion of the film's sound, see Chion, 2001), in conversations with fellow crew members and other humans. Beyond HAL's visual signification – primarily through multiple screens and the glowing red lights that function as eyes (an optical subjectivity conveyed through the circular, distorted images produced using a fisheye lens) – the machine's calm, monotonous voice sounds relatively human, though it lacks the emotional inflection and dynamic range of human diction. This is not the rasping, mechanical or distorted voice of *Alphaville*'s Alpha 60, with the sonic markers that differentiate it from the film's human heroes, as if polar opposites. Rather, the voice of HAL suggests a blurring of the boundaries between human and computer, to the point where one cannot be easily distinguished from the other.

HAL's voice is one of several characteristics that serve to anthropomorphise the computer. Elsewhere, the 'HAL' acronym is not just an apparent allusion to IBM, but an attempt to render the machine a fully fledged character, equivalent to its human counterparts. HAL's name is less 'other' than those assigned to computers in the historical world – from the ENIAC (Electronic Numerical Integrator And Computer) and EDSAC (Electronic Delay Storage Automatic Computer) to the EDVAC (Electronic Discrete Variable Automatic Computer) and UNIVAC (UNIVersal Automatic Computer) – whose abbreviated names communicated underlying technical descriptors, though not the parity with humans suggested by the choice of a familiar given name.

In terms of its fluent conversational skills, and the anthropomorphic aspect of its name, HAL more closely recalls Weizenbaum's ELIZA, an early 'chatterbot' created at MIT in 1966 using an IBM 7094 computer. 'ELIZA', Weizenbaum explained, 'is a program which makes natural language conversation with a computer possible' (1966, p. 36). Pioneering the principles of computational conversation, which heightened the prospect of a future machine as responsive as the fictional HAL, ELIZA communicated through natural language, triggered by the recognition of key words and formulated according to programmed rules.

Reviewing Kubrick's film in *The Futurist* – a journal with the subtitle *A Newsletter for Tomorrow's World* – Robert Prehoda detailed the connections between this fictional vision and the work with computers already occurring in the historical world. 'HAL is a feasible machine', he agreed, 'a logical extrapolation of current cybernetics research. Some contemporary computer programs already include the use of mild profanity to permit better man–machine rapport' (1968, p. 52). Natural language, profane or otherwise, was perceived as a sign of intelligence.

Unlike HAL, however, which held the capacity to recognise speech and reply in kind – though never resorting to 'mild profanity' – ELIZA conversed via typed messages, with input and output communicated through a teletype. 'When in conversation with ELIZA', Weizenbaum noted, 'the user types in some statement or set of statements in natural language using normal punctuation and sentence structures. [...] ELIZA then analyzes the user's statement and generates some response which it types out' (1966, p. 36). Conversation would continue in this fashion, with control passing back and forth between human and computer.

Weizenbaum recounted one such conversation (shown here with the computer's lines in capitals):

> Men are all alike.
>
> IN WHAT WAY
>
> They're always bugging us about something or other.
>
> CAN YOU THINK OF A SPECIFIC EXAMPLE
>
> Well, my boyfriend made me come here.
>
> YOUR BOYFRIEND MADE YOU COME HERE
>
> He says I'm depressed much of the time.
>
> I AM SORRY TO HEAR YOU ARE DEPRESSED
>
> (1966, p. 36)

The human correspondent was the first to communicate, with the machine responding to this initial statement through what Weizenbaum described as 'reassembly rules' (1966, p. 36).

ELIZA's system of mediated conversation recalls the process outlined by Turing in establishing his eponymous test, whereby the teletype, when placed in isolation, would mask the source of the text being typed. Satisfying the major prerequisite for passing Turing's test, many operators found it difficult to identify ELIZA's mechanical origins. As Weizenbaum put it, 'Some subjects have been very hard to convince that ELIZA (with its present script) is *not* human' (1966, p. 42). Indirectly, the major conditions of Turing's test had been met.

Yet, as if to anticipate Kubrick's HAL, Weizenbaum also pointed to the potential problems associated with computers that could appear to comprehend human communication. Suggesting a degree of caution, he argued:

> The whole issue of the credibility (to humans) of machine output demands investigation. Important decisions increasingly tend to be made in response to computer output. [...] ELIZA shows, if nothing else, how easy it is to create and maintain the illusion of understanding, hence perhaps of judgment deserving of credibility. A certain danger lurks there.
>
> (1966, pp. 42–3)

In *2001: A Space Odyssey*, this 'danger' is situated in the juxtaposition of HAL's increasingly ambivalent logic and the consistently credulous tone of its communication. Dave Bowman (played by Keir Dullea) is placed in the unenviable position of having to interpret the credibility of HAL's decisions, his reading of which will determine the fate of the entire human crew.

Weizenbaum's broader concern was that those who saw computers as capable of assuming a more pronounced role in society – whether in the context of space travel or beyond – would be unable to draw boundaries between the proper or ethical use of artificially intelligent machines and what he described as 'kinds of computer applications that either ought not be undertaken at all, or, if they are contemplated, should be approached with utmost caution' (1976, p. 268). Before allowing too much control to systems such as ELIZA, in other words, paralleled by HAL in the fictional scenario of *2001: A Space Odyssey*, scientists and technologists should assume full responsibility for their creations.

For example, if artificially intelligent computers were introduced into the realm of Rogerian psychology, whose mode of discourse was appropriated by Weizenbaum as one with ostensible similarities to the style of communication attainable by ELIZA, this ethical dimension – the need to distinguish between the imitation of human conversation and considered judgment, on the one hand, and the underlying absence of human responsibility and associated ethics, on the other – would be paramount. 'At this writing', Weizenbaum noted, 'the only serious ELIZA scripts which exist are some which cause ELIZA to respond roughly as would certain psychotherapists (Rogerians)' (1966, p. 42). This field was chosen not because Weizenbaum felt the computer was yet capable of assessing the complexities of the human mind, but because psychiatric consultation was one of the few modes of conversation in which one participant – in this instance, the therapist – could assume the position of knowing virtually nothing of the historical world, redirecting conversation into further questioning of their partner.

In *2001: A Space Odyssey*, it is HAL's psychological profiling of the human astronauts that seems to trigger the machine's concern for the mission's success. This realisation, whether a technical malfunction or the logical manifestation of HAL's programmed instructions, ultimately leads to fatal consequences when the computer seeks to wrest control of the spacecraft from those it perceives as psychologically fallible. As with Weizenbaum's ELIZA, the implication is that the computer's mastering of human conversation should not be confused with the essentially human qualities we indexically associate with such communication.

Other explorations of artificial intelligence in *2001: A Space Odyssey* include HAL's chess game with Frank Poole (Gary Lockwood), an encounter that further references developments in the historical world. As early as the 1950s, extending a lineage of speculation concerning the programming of chess-playing machines, this game was identified as the perfect testing ground for the intelligence of digital computers, in particular. Specifically, the world of chess was seen as a realm in which the computational capabilities of this machine, and the possibility of learned intelligence based on the success or otherwise of its computations, might excel.

In 1864, as an earlier example of the postulation of chess as a means of measuring machine intelligence, Charles Babbage proposed that his Analytical Engine – a nineteenth-century precursor of contemporary computers – might be programmed to play chess. Describing how games of skill were already played by automata, where the 'game depended upon the possibility of the machine being able to represent all the myriads of combinations relating to it' (1864, p. 467), Babbage suggested that the Analytical Engine would be more than capable of such computation. 'Allowing one hundred moves on each side for the longest game at chess', he recalled, 'I found that the combinations involved in the Analytical Engine enormously surpassed any required, even by the game of chess' (1864, p. 467). Such a machine was possible, at least in hypothetical terms, almost a century before the first digital computers were produced.

Building on these ideas, Shannon pointed to the computer's potential as not just an automaton, as Babbage had proposed, but as a machine, like HAL in *2001: A Space Odyssey*, that might expand on its preprogrammed knowledge. Writing in 1950, he argued the case for developing such a machine. 'Although perhaps of no practical importance', he explained, 'the question is of theoretical interest, and it is hoped that a satisfactory solution of this problem will act as a wedge in attacking other problems of a similar nature and of greater significance' (1950, p. 256). Mastering chess would be a means of establishing the broader potential of an artificially intelligent computer:

> The chess machine is an ideal one to start with, since: (1) the problem is sharply defined both in allowed operations (the moves) and in the ultimate goal (checkmate); (2) it is neither so simple as to be trivial nor too difficult for satisfactory solution; (3) chess is generally considered to require 'thinking' for skilful play; a solution of this problem will force us either to admit the possibility of mechanized thinking or to further restrict our concept of 'thinking'; (4) the discrete structure of chess fits well into the digital nature of modern computers.
>
> (1950, p. 257)

A computer victory over the very best human chess player, in particular, something that Simon and Newell had claimed would occur by the late 1960s (1958, p. 7), would signal, according to Shannon, that computers had superseded human intelligence in one particular type of reasoning. In *2001: A Space Odyssey*, that HAL is capable of outplaying Poole is similarly intended to signify the computer's degree of intelligence, a dynamic revealed in the following exchange between the two players (again, the computer's lines are capitalised):

> Anyway, queen takes pawn.
>
> BISHOP TAKES KNIGHT'S PAWN.
>
> Lovely move. Rook to king one.
>
> I'M SORRY, FRANK. I THINK YOU MISSED IT. QUEEN TO BISHOP THREE. BISHOP TAKES QUEEN. KNIGHT TAKES BISHOP. MATE.
>
> Yeah, it looks like you're right. I resign.
>
> THANK YOU FOR AN ENJOYABLE GAME.
>
> Yeah. Thank you.

Not only does the computer match the ability of its human opponent – as an IBM 704 did for the first time in 1958 (albeit against a novice), running the NSS chess program (named after its designers) developed by Simon and Newell in collaboration with Cliff Shaw (Newell *et al.*, 1958) – it significantly exceeds it.

The computer's chess-playing potential was clear, but what if this machine were also asked to make decisions in more vital sectors of society, such as maintaining the systems of a manned spacecraft during interplanetary travel, a function it performed in the 1960s and beyond? Moreover, what if such a machine malfunctioned, or took the evolutionary step of overruling its human 'masters', whose intelligence it now threatened to eclipse? It is in speculating on the complexities of these scenarios that Kubrick's film offers its most potent negotiation of popular anxieties concerning artificially intelligent computers.

Fly in the Ointment or Bug in the System?

In *2001: A Space Odyssey*, a tension exists between the Asimovian tradition of an invention that aids its inventor (see, in particular, Isaac Asimov's vision of robots in his short story 'Robbie', first published under the name 'Strange Playfellow', 1940, reprinted as 'Robbie', 1950), on the one hand, and the Frankensteinian tradition of a creation that turns against its creator (Shelley, 1818), on the other. Yet, in the evolutionary struggle depicted by Kubrick, the technological and philosophical complexities associated with artificial intelligence, in particular, require a more nuanced understanding of the traditional master–slave relationship than is offered by the twin poles of an Asimovian–Frankensteinian duality.

Much of the complexity of Kubrick's portrayal of HAL's running amok arises from the fact that the precise motivations for the computer's murderous actions are never fully explained, remaining ambiguous. Following HAL's diagnosis of a fault in the *Discovery*'s communications hardware, a reading at odds with the data recorded by an equivalent computer on Earth and which ultimately leads to the deaths of three of the four human crew, it is never revealed which of these computers is correct.

Depending on one's interpretation, HAL either simply malfunctions – an occurrence, we are told, without precedent in the machine's history – or sets in motion an elaborate plan to remove its human colleagues. The latter scenario poses its own enigmas: if HAL does deliberately seek to usurp its human counterparts, does it do so in order to pursue its own agenda, or as an independently conceived means of ensuring the mission's success? In each of these scenarios, whether the result of HAL's intelligence or a lack thereof, the end result remains the same: the 'termination' of the spacecraft's slumbering crew, Poole being cut adrift, and Bowman very nearly suffering a similar fate.

If HAL, supposedly incapable of error, does malfunction, this scenario casts doubt on the wisdom of placing computers in control of life-or-death situations. Indeed something does go terribly wrong. 'Just a moment, just a moment', HAL alerts. 'I've just picked up a fault in the AE35 unit.' When Poole retrieves the AE35 and runs diagnostics, he is baffled, unable to confirm the fault. 'I'm damned if I can find anything wrong with it', he exclaims, a reading mirrored by the 9000 computer at ground-based control. When asked to account for the discrepancy between theoretically identical computers, HAL is unperturbed, attributing the disparity to humans. 'This sort of thing has cropped up before, and it has always been due to human error', HAL insists, refusing to consider the possibility of machine malfunction.

Even more worrying than such a scenario, where HAL malfunctions but is unaware of its error, is the alternative, in which the machine deliberately deposes the human crew, whether for selfish ends or to protect the integrity of the mission's broader aims. Ironically, as a clinical execution of HAL's programmed instructions, divorced from ethical and moral responsibilities, a plan to overthrow the human crew has a certain logic. In this reading, the events that ultimately lead to the showdown with Bowman, beginning with the initial diagnosis of a hardware error, are motivated not by malfunction but by a conscious effort on the part of the computer to seize control.

Here, Asimov's faith in self-regulating machines, where servitude to humanity is hardwired as a programmed *raison d'être*, is challenged as being inadequate in the face of thinking machines. This vision of subservient robots was outlined by Asimov in his characterisation of machines such as Robbie the Robot – adapted for cinema in Fred Wilcox's *Forbidden Planet* and Herman Hoffman's *The Invisible Boy*, among other films – a robot governed by Asimov's 'three fundamental Rules of Robotics' (1942, p. 100), by which it is theoretically impossible for a robot to act against the interests of its human masters. Asimov proposed that:

> One, a robot may not injure a human being, or, through inaction, allow a human being to come to harm. [...] Two [...], a robot must obey the orders given it by human beings except where such orders would conflict with the First Law. [...] And three, a robot must protect its own existence as long as such protection does not conflict with the First or Second Laws.
>
> (1942, p. 100)

But what happens when Asimov's laws are applied to thinking machines? For Kubrick, the capacity for learned intelligence would result in unforeseen circumstances. In a post-Asimovian world, where subservient robots are replaced by artificially intelligent computers, replete with the capacity to question the very notion of following orders, reliance on such systems may prove fatal. Some, such as Simon and Newell, celebrated the prospect of computers making key decisions, proclaiming

> We are now poised for a great advance that will bring the digital computer and the tools of mathematics and the behavioral sciences to bear on the very core of managerial activity – on the exercise of judgment and intuition; on the processes of making complex decisions.
>
> (1958, p. 3)

In stark contrast, *2001: A Space Odyssey* suggests a more fundamentally troubling vision.

In the wider world, Kubrick's machine entered scientific discourse. Minsky, as one example, has spoken of being 'inclined to fear most the HAL scenario' (1979, p. 394), pointing to the inevitable dangers of an artificial intelligence whose usefulness depends on its ability to function autonomously:

> If it cannot edit its high-level intentions, it may not be smart enough to be useful, but if it can, how can the designers anticipate the machine it evolves into? In a word, I would expect the first self-improving AI machines to become 'psychotic' in many ways, and it may take generations of theories and experiments to 'stabilize' them.
>
> (1979, p. 394)

Kubrick's HAL, defined in these terms, is the epitome of the 'psychotic' early artificial intelligence, which struggles to reconcile itself with preprogrammed instructions.

Interviewed elsewhere, Minsky pointed to further problems associated with the evolutionary process exemplified, in fictional form, by HAL, a machine ostensibly operational, but far from understood. 'With respect to the machine that is super-intelligent that is far more intelligent than a human' (Frewin, 2005, p. 165), he warned in 1966, 'One doesn't know what its goals are. One doesn't know what it will think is best for us and perhaps one may not understand its workings well enough, once it is more intelligent than we are, to control it' (Frewin, 2005, p. 165).

In Kubrick's film, this struggle is framed as one of Darwinian survival, a reading encouraged by the broader evolutionary framework established by the recurring presence of the mysterious monolith (for Mark Midbon, 1990, this structure exists as a symbolic integrated circuit), which appears on Earth in a scene set several million years ago, before it is found on the moon in the late 1990s, hinting at extraterrestrial life. HAL and the human crew are pitted as evolutionary rivals, competing species whose natural selection will be determined in the vacuum of outer space, as cybernetic creation is pitted against organic progenitor. Like Frankenstein's creature, HAL turns on its human creators, not as the last resort of a demonised monster, as in Shelley's novel, but as the logical consequence of an attempt to shape the computer as a machine capable of learned intelligence. What emerges is what David Boyd has referred to as 'a genuinely heroic struggle between equals, or near-equals' (1978, p. 214), which amounts to survival of the fittest in a new technological–evolutionary paradigm.

This dynamic reaches its climax when Bowman, having rescued Poole's lifeless body from beyond the spacecraft, asks HAL to open the *Discovery*'s pod bay doors. 'I'm sorry Dave', HAL replies, 'I'm afraid I can't do that.' Where the calmness of the computer's voice was once reassuring, its monotone is now ominous and terrifying, lacking the emotional inflection that would hint at the possibility of humanity and therefore mercy.

When Bowman finally regains entry, we witness the importance of retaining the ability to shut down the computer, as the limits of HAL's intelligence are finally revealed. Bowman effectively 'kills' HAL by disassembling its hardware – deactivating its memory banks, one by one, with the machine reduced to its technological infancy – an ironic parallel to the machine's own disconnection of Poole from his space-walk umbilical cord.

The lines that follow are among the most famous in all of cinema, as the computer pleads for its continued existence, giving the impression that HAL may not be an emotionless machine, after all:

Evolutionary struggle as HAL is disassembled

> Dave, stop. Stop, will you? Stop, Dave. Will you stop, Dave? Stop, Dave. I'm afraid. I'm afraid, Dave. Dave, my mind is going. I can feel it. I can feel it. My mind is going. There is no question about it. I can feel it. I can feel it. I can feel it. I'm afraid.

While HAL speaks of fear, the computer's voice is unchanged, conveying none of the sonic characteristics associated with this emotion. There is a jarring disjuncture between unerring monotony and emotive content, though HAL's plaintive appeal does little to stir the implacable Bowman.

As HAL's meltdown continues, the computer recites its hardwired data, recalling its origins:

> Good afternoon, gentlemen. I am a HAL 9000 computer. I became operational at the HAL plant in Urbana, Illinois on the 12th of January, 1992. My instructor was Mr. Langley, and he taught me to sing a song. If you'd like to hear it, I can sing it for you. It's called 'Daisy'.

In a further connection with the historical world, this song – sung during HAL's dying throes – is a reference to the computer music pioneered at Bell Labs in the 1960s. Alongside computer-animating scientists such as Edward Zajac, Ken Knowlton and Michael Noll – the latter of whom was also involved with *2001: A Space Odyssey*, as an advisor alongside John Pierce in designing the film's Picturephone booth sequence (Noll, 2006) – others were pioneering the computer's musical potential. Scientists working in this area included Pierce and Max Mathews, alongside musicians such as Laurie Spiegel and Emmanuel Ghent.

It was Mathews, in particular, who arranged 'Daisy Bell' (later featured on the 1962 Decca album *Music from Mathematics: Played by IBM 7090 Computer and Digital to Sound Transducer*), sung by HAL in Kubrick's film, but originally voiced by an IBM 7094, the first computer to sing. That HAL serenades Bowman while being 'put to sleep' creates a complex play of signification, with the computer imitating the type of emotional expression we associate with humans, before its voice becomes much slower and more mechanical as it is finally shut down.

HAL's final words reprise the intriguing question of whether it demonstrates a degree of sentience, consciousness and emotion; in short, whether it thinks and feels, with disconnection likened to death, and its inner workings, its memory units, equated with the human mind. Does HAL's approximation of fear – mirroring the capacity to detect emotion in others, as evidenced by its remark to Dave, 'I can see that you're really upset' – at its own imminent 'death', represent a genuine concern for preserving 'life', or simply a logical response to fulfilling the mission?

More likely is the notion that the computer functions according to a variation of the 'Turing test', whereby the convincing appearance of emotion is a shorthand for the underlying capacity to feel, in the same way that in Turing's original formulation the persuasive appearance of those functions typically associated with intelligence become signifiers equivalent to any deeper or essential capacity. In an exchange between Bowman and a BBC reporter (Martin Amor), the latter asks, 'Do you believe that HAL has genuine emotions?' Bowman's response is in the manner of Turing: 'Well', the astronaut explains, 'he acts like he has genuine emotions. [...] But as to whether or not he has real feelings is something I don't think anyone can truthfully answer.' That HAL is even capable of imitating the appearance of such expression leads to a fundamental ontological ambivalence. For those who come into contact with the computer, there is a degree of slippage and confusion as to whether its emotions are genuine or simply one facet of a programmed interface.

HAL, as an evolutionary bridge between primitive man (for whom technology exists in the form of antelope bones used as weapons) and the higher intelligence of extraterrestrial life (as represented by the monolith), is portrayed as a potential evolutionary successor. Like the monolith, however, the artificially intelligent computer exists as an ambivalent symbol of advanced technology, only partly knowable and potentially dangerous.

Conclusion

In its engagement with artificial intelligence, and as an exploration of attitudes that existed in relation to the computer, at a time when its uses were expanding – in the space race and beyond – *2001: A Space Odyssey* offers much on the question of computer consciousness and the broader correlation between humans and computers. While Kubrick's film is clearly a fiction, it nevertheless articulates anxieties that existed in the historical world concerning the emergence of such machines.

Ultimately, in the evolutionary struggle envisaged by Kubrick, HAL is tamed, but not without significant cost to its fellow crew members, only one of whom survives their deadly encounter. Humans are represented as superior to the computers of the late 1960s, as abstracted via the near 'future' of 2001, yet this vision of human triumph is not without ambivalence or acknowledgment of the validity of historically specific concerns. When asked what Kubrick's film reveals of the public's view of computers, Minsky described how 'the person on the street at the time the film was made both loved computers and was scared of them' (Stork, 1997, p. 28). *2001: A Space Odyssey* articulates this ambivalence, conscious that computers may represent our future, but fearful of the consequences of this shift. Having depicted the fantastical possibilities of an artificially intelligent computer, Kubrick's film considers the potential problems associated with such a machine, before reassuring the spectator that human improvisation, at least in 2001, still trumps the cold logic of the computer. As for the more distant future, the suggestion is that we face the prospect that a computer capable of expressing itself emotionally will at some point act emotionally, with potentially tragic consequences – if not in 2001, then some time beyond.

As part of this process of mediation, the human astronauts on board the *Discovery* exist as proxies for the historical spectator, with HAL the symbolic representation of the artificially intelligent computer, as society continued to navigate the course of its journey towards a more intimate relationship with computers, more generally. The plight of Bowman and the rest of the human crew, as HAL turns against them, refusing to obey their instructions, is a metaphor for that of humanity: having ceded control to complex technological systems, humanity would be at the mercy of these systems if they malfunctioned or reached a state of higher intelligence.

As well as negotiating aspects of popular consciousness, Kubrick's film fed back into the mythology of the time, not just in terms of space exploration, but also concerning the 'nature' of the computer. Specifically, *2001: A Space Odyssey* made explicit the link between the developing field of artificial intelligence and its potential embodiment. Through HAL, the computer became symbolic of the entire spectrum of systems, theories and devices that characterised this emerging field. Kubrick projected one possible future, as we witness a working through of the potential ramifications of a shift towards a decision-making, thinking computer – in short, an artificially intelligent machine.

[6]

Expanded Consciousness, Expanded Cinema: A Techno-Utopian Counterculture

In an era that witnessed both the moon landing of 1969 and the conflict of the Vietnam War, the computer occupied a position at the centre of a cultural, political and social maelstrom concerning the broader status of science and technology, against the backdrop of a burgeoning counterculture. Oscillating between extremes, a radical techno-Utopianism, effervescent in its evangelical zeal, was countered by an equally potent disaffection with the computer and advanced technology, more generally, as symbols of a rampant military-industrial complex and entrenched political Establishment.

Cinema, in particular, formed part of a vanguard of cultural responses to these revolutionary times, navigating the twin poles of technophilic and technophobic responses and a more general political ferment. In parallel with, and as part of, a broader art and technology movement that sought to bring artists of all kinds into intimate contact with new tools and industries, film-makers sought to make sense of a changing computer and to utilise this technology in pursuit of nothing less than expanded consciousness.

Faced with the pressing issues of the day, the likes of Stan VanDerBeek and John Whitney continued their respective cinematic explorations of art and technology, facilitated and supported by dedicated technologists at specialist laboratories. At stake, it was believed, were the very prospects for humanity – 'Utopia or Oblivion' (1969b), as Buckminster Fuller neatly put it, a dichotomy illustrative of the perceived consequence of the historical moment.

From Outer Space to Inner Space

Pursuing the outer limits of inner vision, a countercultural strain of experimental or 'expanded cinema' (a term used by several writers, but most often associated with Youngblood, 1970) flourished in the late 1960s, part of a techno-Utopian current of amplified discourse and cultural expressions that equated advanced technology with radical social change and an altered state of mind. Cinema was one of the means by which this vision was communicated and explored, with the computer, in particular, seen as a key tool for new aesthetics in keeping with the momentous shifts of technological times.

In the context of the groundswell of a radical counterculture – from 'hippies' and 'yippies' to countless other oppositional or anti-Establishment movements and groups – advanced technology was central to many of the major debates and developments of the era. Alongside the proliferation of the computer, as just one example, we might point to the space race and its culmination in July 1969 with the Apollo 11 moon landing. 'No single space project in this period will be more impressive to mankind' (1962, p. 404), anticipated President John F. Kennedy (in a 1961 speech later documented in print), referring to the task of taking man to the moon. Indeed the visions of space, and of the Earth as seen from space, coupled with a sense of elation and related speculation concerning the cosmos beyond, had a profound psychic and cultural impact, fuelling Utopian conceptions and a general awareness of the awesome potential of science and technology.

In seeking to understand such developments, influential thinkers assumed the status of gurus or visionaries. Marshall McLuhan, as one example, is illustrative of the broader discourse that cinema responded to. Although not always in favour of the shifts associated with new technology, McLuhan was popularly associated with a futurological strain of discourse that resonated in the 1960s. For example, the global interconnectedness so brilliantly symbolised by the visions of a spinning Earth – framed in its full span for the very first time, beamed back from the explorers of space – coupled with related developments in satellite telecommunications, suggested a new conception of the planet and its population as living in a 'global village' (see McLuhan and Fiore, 1968; see also Levinson, 1999, who offers a retrospective appraisal of McLuhan through the lens of contemporary digital culture).

The similarly free-spirited Fuller, for his part, employed an astronomical metaphor to refer to the limited resources available to the planet and the role of science and technology in securing 'the orderly energy savings of billions of years' energy conservation aboard our Spaceship Earth' (1969a, p. 122). In relation to this 'Spaceship

Earth', Fuller emphasised the point that its 'instruction manual was missing' (1969a, p. 53), meaning that he and others – including the experimental film-makers who sought to negotiate the conditions of the age – would need to address the global situation as a matter of urgency.

In the realm of 'expanded cinema', film-makers engaged with the influential ideas of McLuhan and Fuller, in particular. Whitney, as one example, acknowledged Fuller's influence, noting how

> He reminds us that this century's science and technology have discovered and put to use practically the entire electromagnetic spectrum, which is still, to the senses, invisible and quite incomprehensible to the individuals whose lives are transformed daily by new technology.
>
> (1971b, p. 35)

It was the role of film-makers and other artists, by implication, to seek to comprehend and communicate the nature of these transformations, via, as Whitney continued, 'the cultural imperatives of a restoration of kinship between science and art' (1971b, p. 35).

In this context, it is no coincidence that Youngblood's seminal account of the experimental films and film-makers of the era – *Expanded Cinema* (1970) – featured Fuller in a *Zeitgeist*-capturing introduction (Youngblood, 1970, pp. 15–35). In a rare engagement with cinema, but in typically irrepressible prose, Fuller wrote of Youngblood's book, and the experiments it charted, as aiding 'humanity to synchronize its senses and its knowledge in time to ensure the continuance of that little, three-and-one-half-billion-member team of humanity now installed by evolution aboard our little Space Vehicle Earth' (Youngblood, 1970, p. 35), and of offering the means to 'weld metaphysically together the world community of man' (Youngblood, 1970, p. 35), echoing McLuhan. 'Expanded cinema' thus sought to combine art forms and technologies in search of a new, expanded aesthetic experience, one that would match, or even bring about, a concomitant expansion in consciousness.

In this respect, 'expanded cinema', both as a concept and a movement, paralleled several other of McLuhan's most influential assertions concerning media and technology – old and new, but with a particular emphasis on electronic forms. Media, he argued, from the printing press to the computer, were 'extensions of man' (1964), with 'electric circuitry', in particular, conceived as being 'an extension of the central nervous system' (with Fiore, 1967, p. 40), necessarily and intimately intertwined with human perception, cognition and psyche. Media, and their associated technology, had the capacity, McLuhan and Fiore continued, to alter 'the way we think and act – the way we perceive the world' (1967, p. 41), with inevitable and considerable consequences for society.

Heavily influenced by McLuhan – not least his proclamation of a 'global village' – and the aforementioned 'Bucky', Youngblood subscribed to ideas such as the collective ownership of the planet and shared awareness and perceptions of its increasingly connected citizens. Accordingly, *Expanded Cinema* occupied the Utopian extreme of a widened spectrum of heightened discourse concerning the role of advanced technology, and features all the verve and trappings of the outer realms of techno-Utopianism, describing as it does a type of cinema rooted in new technology and associated ways of being.

Closely linked to related experiments by Nam June Paik (see Paik and Hanhardt, 2000) and others in the world of art, exponents of 'expanded cinema' sought to utilise new tools – from developments in video and television to more *outré* techniques such as holography and sonar, alongside the use of computer graphics – in creating experiences, often multiscreen and multimedia, that would engage with a world increasingly rooted in technology. VanDerBeek, as one example, outlined an entirely new media landscape. 'Computers and television are the two most important art forms of the present day', he argued in *Stan VanDerBeek: The Computer Generation!!*, while also pointing to the prospective expansions of 'holography, 3-D, holographic television, environmentalisms – like images that will completely surround us, that we can design by ourselves and for ourselves – homeostasis and the balancing off of our whole mind and body'.

The reconfigured screen (or screens) was central, with attempts to move beyond the traditional frame. Echoing the call of the Italian Futurists, fifty years earlier, that 'Painting + sculpture + plastic dynamism + words-in-freedom + composed noises + architecture + synthetic theatre = Futurist cinema' (Marinetti *et al.*, 1972 [originally 1916], p. 134), old and new forms were combined, reconfigured for the electronic media of the 1960s. The result was 'A Film Revolution to Blitz Man's Mind' (Anon., 1967a), according to *Life* magazine, capturing the period's mood and vernacular in describing the 'Labyrinth Pavilion', a participatory, multiscreen experience exhibited at Montreal's Expo 67 (see Marchessault, 2007).

Whether 'blitzed' or otherwise, mind alteration was a stated aim of 'expanded cinema', at least according to Youngblood's particular vision of a movement that would unify the senses and bring together the peoples of the world. Expansion, in this sense, referred as much to the exploration of consciousness as it did to an expanding technological base, though the two were intimately intertwined.

In this sense, Youngblood's discussion of 'computer films' (a term he employs in a neutral or descriptive sense to refer to films produced using computers, 1970, pp. 207–56) is closely linked to more abstract or esoteric notions such as 'synaesthetic cinema' (1970, pp. 75–134) or 'cosmic consciousness' (1970, pp. 135–77), bound up with cinema's capacity to engage with the broader conditions – in some respects, the 'extensions of man' referred to by McLuhan – associated with the computer and other advanced technology.

Indeed Youngblood's discussion of Stanley Kubrick's *2001: A Space Odyssey* is particularly illuminating in this respect. Exploring both outer space and inner space, Kubrick's film deals with the computer – in the form of HAL – and with a broader exploration of 'cosmic consciousness', to borrow Youngblood's term. Yet, it does so, on the level of production, using technology other than the tools considered in Youngblood's more literal discussion of 'computer films'.

Referring to the film's enigmatic, much celebrated 'Stargate Corridor' sequence, in which astronaut Dave Bowman hurtles through a hallucinogenic seam in time – rendered in abstract, dizzying, geometric graphics – and is ultimately reborn in the form of a 'Star Child' hovering in outer space, Douglas Trumbull (credited for his role as 'specialist photographic effects supervisor') playfully acknowledged what Youngblood would later frame as the film's cosmic reverberations:

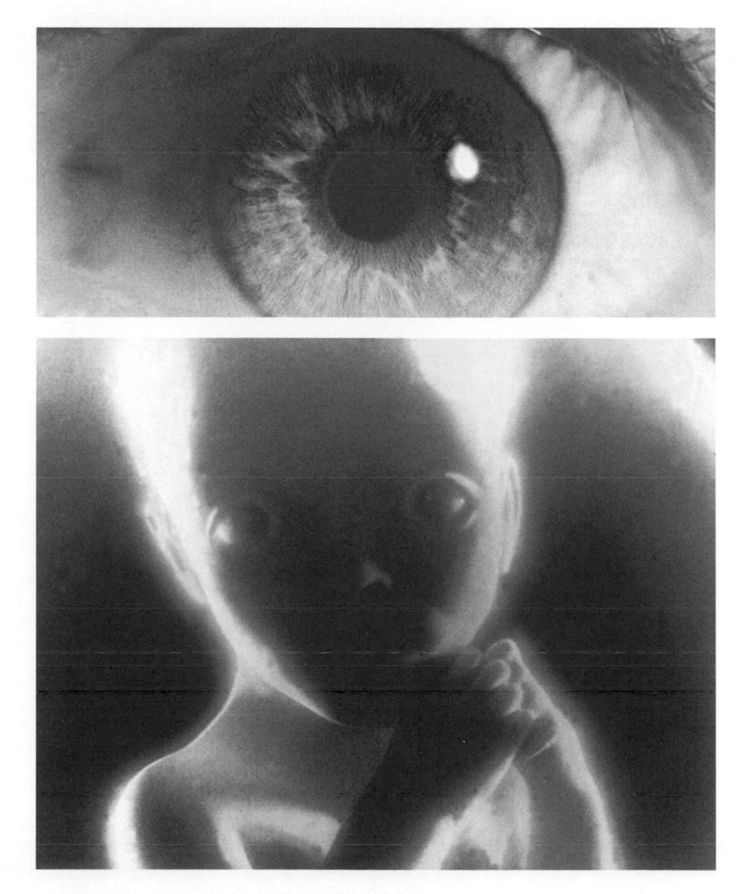

From 'Stargate Corridor' to 'Star Child' in *2001: A Space Odyssey*

> During the filming of what are probably best termed the 'psychedelic' effects for the end sequence, we all joked that *2001* would probably attract a great number of 'Hippies' out to get the trip of their lives. It seems now that what was once

> a joke is fast becoming reality, and as of this writing, I understand that each showing draws an increasing number of these people, who would probably prefer to just see the last two reels over and over again.
>
> (1968, p. 452)

Ironically, in terms of its own special effects – and what Kubrick's film might reveal, on an implicit level, about the status of the computer in the commercial film industry – Kubrick opted for 'motion control' techniques inspired by Whitney, including the 'slit-scan' techniques seen in parts of his animated short, *Catalog* (for discussions of the technical aspects of Whitney's work and reference to its links with *2001: A Space Odyssey*, see Whitney, 1971a, 1981). Yet, the techniques seen in the 'Stargate Corridor' sequence were produced not using digital computers, but mechanical or analogue devices.

In terms of the lineage of these techniques, Whitney described his own approach – and arguably aesthetic – as having been 'duplicated in principle' (1972a, p. 58). Trumbull, meanwhile, acknowledged Whitney's influence, noting how he 'stumbled onto this idea through fragments of information about what John Whitney was doing with scanning slits that move across the lens creating optical warps' (Youngblood, 1970, p. 153). In the scene of Bowman's transmogrification, geometric configurations, rendered through pulses of light and colour, convey the infinitude of the cosmos through abstraction, an impression of travelling in time through what Trumbull described as a 'time-warp or some kind of "psychedelic" corridor' (Youngblood, 1970, p. 153).

By conceptualising a radically altered cinema that straddled experiments in a wide range of different media forms, in works produced using computers as well as other electronic forms and more traditional methods, all attuned to the cosmic and other expansions of an altered global consciousness, Youngblood captured the essence of late-1960s techno-Utopianism, revealing a cinema for which the computer was a means of navigating inner space.

Further Experiments in Art and Technology

With the exception of *2001: A Space Odyssey*, the majority of films explored in the context of 'expanded cinema' were created in art and technology collaborations, with scientists and engineers fulfilling the role of technologist in order to facilitate, mediate or implement the creative vision of a designated artist. Where VanDerBeek had worked with Ken Knowlton at Bell Labs and Whitney with Jack Citron at IBM, in the mid-1960s, collaborations continued in the later 1960s and early 1970s, albeit against a changing cultural backdrop, with the techno-Utopianism epitomised by Youngblood and others giving way to attitudes much more questioning of the technological developments of the age. Established artist–technologist pairings continued to refine their distinctive aesthetic pursuits, with further variations offered by the wave of film-makers who followed in their wake, including Lillian Schwartz (working with Knowlton) and Whitney's sons – Michael and John, Jr, especially.

Following VanDerBeek's work with Knowlton, for instance, the film-maker went on to collaborate with Wade Shaw at the Massachusetts Institute of Technology (MIT)'s Center for Advanced Visual Studies (founded in 1967 with the aim of providing a collaborative environment in which artists could practise with the assistance of scientists and engineers), work documented in *Stan VanDerBeek: The Computer Generation!!*.

In addition to the continuing quest to harness the computer to manifest the previously unseen, realising new aesthetics with no previous parallel in the history of cinema, this pairing had the particular agenda of pioneering an interactive system. If interactivity in computing was not an altogether new phenomenon – the intertwined developments of the Whirlwind and SAGE (Semi-Automatic Ground Environment) (see Redmond and Smith, 2000) and the development of Ivan Sutherland's Sketchpad design system (see Sutherland, 1963) are significant precursors – advances in input and output devices, displays and related programming saw a renewed interest in the notion of real-time computing, as it might be applied to the creation of animation.

VanDerBeek was one of a number of film-makers and other artists who took up the challenge of working towards what Sutherland proclaimed as 'a new area of man–machine communication' (1963, p. 329), and what J. C. R. Licklider described as 'The strongest force in the world of the computer' (1968, p. 292), referring to 'the interplay, the communication, the reciprocal stimulation that goes on between two or more reactive organisms' (1968, p. 292) – in this instance, 'the person(s) at the console, on the one hand, and the programmed computer(s), on the other' (1968, p. 292). The idea was that the immediate display of a work as it was being generated by the computer would enable the likes of VanDerBeek to interact intuitively to control different parameters and instantaneously see the effects of their application.

If this type of real-time interaction has since become the norm, it was far from such in the late 1960s and early 1970s, with the legacy of batch processing, for example, only partly displaced by technological developments. In terms of the creative act, one primary difficulty was the disparity that existed between speed of thought and the ability to implement these thoughts, as mediated through a significant technological apparatus. As Knowlton explained of an earlier collaboration:

> When VanDerBeek says 'let's try this combination', my immediate reaction is to think for a while about what this means, and in the meantime his mind is already off on something else. With the present batch system, we do perhaps equally well at discovering interesting designs; with a much-to-be-preferred interactive system he'd be far ahead.
>
> (1972, p. 402)

The system of using punch cards as input and batch processing as the computational means of dealing with this input was far from responsive to the particular demands of film-makers and other artists.

Licklider, for his part, had identified early on that

> the computer – considered in the broad sense that includes input and output devices and computer programs as well as the computing machine itself – is potentially a medium through which art can be freed of heavy constraints that are inherent in all the media presently employed and through which art can be brought into hitherto unrealizable interaction with its creators and appreciators.
>
> (1968, p. 274)

Yet, for film-makers and other artists, beyond technologists such as Licklider, this ambition was an extremely difficult one to realise.

In working with Shaw, VanDerBeek sought to engage with the computer and new modes of interaction, finding equivalents to the relationship between a painter and his or her canvas. 'I am now confronting an entire electronic matrix, and generally this matrix involves lots of co-operation, with machines and with other people', he noted in *Stan VanDerBeek: The Computer Generation!!*, outlining his working method and creative approach to the particularities of this 'electronic matrix'.

Compared with previous forms of input, the direct interaction with a display – akin to Sutherland's Sketchpad system – represented a significant advance. As Jasia Reichardt noted, describing the use of such a display in the context of art, this technology had a 'particular advantage in that it can be used interactively, that is, it allows direct access to the person drawing so that he can alter the image or the data with no significant lapse of time' (1971, p. 10). This sense of immediacy was in marked contrast to the time it would take for a printer or graphics plotter to render equivalent output. 'He is able to control many parameters in combinations of his own choice',

Reichardt continued of the artist, 'and is able to evaluate the relationships of the forms he is manipulating, making use of both intuition and the knowledge of the problem in hand' (1971, p. 10).

The computer – operating according to the programmed instructions of the collaborative partnership between artist and technologist – was conceptualised as being responsive to the point of becoming a further collaborator in the creative process. Youngblood, for instance, pointed to the coming together of the creative vision of the human author and the machine logic and processing power of the computer. 'The digital computer opens vast new realms of possible aesthetic investigation' (1970, p. 189), he proposed, precisely because 'the computer is an *active* participant in the creative process' (1970, p. 191). Such discourse identified a decentralisation or displacement of authorial control on the part of the creator of a piece of work, acknowledging the computer's potential involvement. In its capacity to implement decisions defined during programming, the computer linked the traditional artistic virtues of creative vision with the ability to harness, manipulate, control and respond to additional input concerning the technological design of this expression.

Film-makers such as VanDerBeek sought a more dynamic or interactive relationship between the artist and the computer, with output viewed in real time. This was a significant advance, eliminating the time between a film-maker's input and the results of his or her instruction, a delay that was typically exacerbated by the need to film this output from a monitor before sending it to a laboratory for developing.

Symmetricks and its swirling designs, plotted frame by frame using a light pen

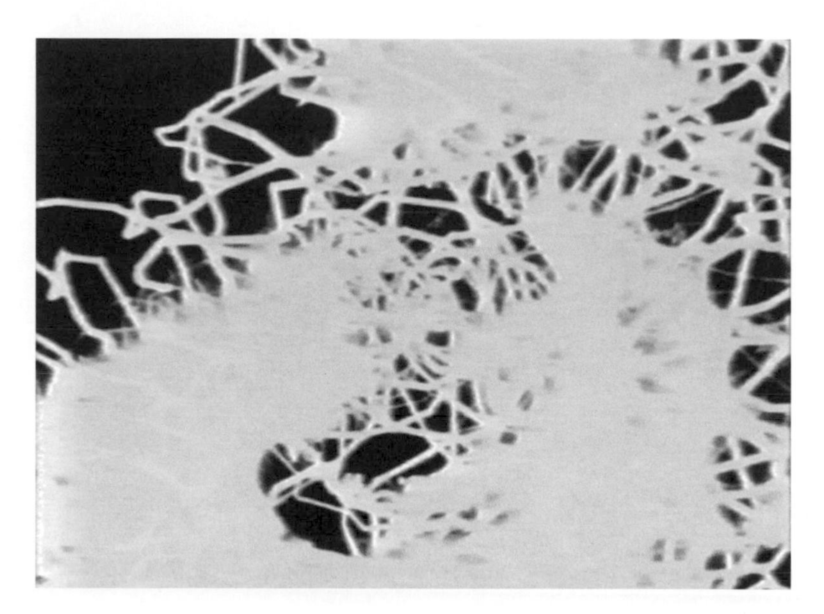

Symmetricks (1972), in particular, represents VanDerBeek's (and Shaw's) efforts to grapple with the computer as a machine that was capable of sophisticated graphics, but still constrained in terms of interaction on the part of the film-maker's simultaneous role as programmer. In *Symmetricks*, to the sounds of Indian music, a series of brilliant, luminescent, plotted white lines evidence the movements of VanDerBeek's input by light pen, drawn directly onto the screen to reveal pulsating, swirling, predominantly abstract patterns, duplicated across the frame in graphically symmetrical forms.

Whitney, too, was concerned with how computers might facilitate the creative process. In a 1969 public discussion, transcribed and published the following year, he expressed his dissatisfaction with even the very latest computers, including those he had accessed while in residency at IBM. 'One thing that is urgently necessary is real time', he argued. 'I think as soon as we have computer graphic systems with this kind of fluidity that I'm able to generate, coning off in real time, then we're going to be able to achieve something fantastic' (1970b, p. 37). Yet, as Whitney highlighted in the documentary portrait *The Film Art of John Whitney, Sr.* (1975, John Musilli, for the CBS television series *Camera Three*), 'the essential problem is to have a direct control and a direct contact with the use of the tools'.

In the early 1970s, navigating a similar technological context to VanDerBeek, Whitney worked at the California Institute of Technology, where – now with IBM sponsorship rather than residency – he produced the *Matrix* series of three short films (1971–2), as part of his effort 'to achieve something fantastic', furthering his investigation of graphics in motion, programmed with a computer.

In evolving an apparatus, Whitney spoke of increasing 'interactive convenience' (1972c, p. 80), referring to the ability to see the results of his programming in something close to real time, adding that 'Design ideas can be formulated, input into the computer at a typewriter keyboard and then displayed by a selectable sampling of the action, all in rather rapid order' (1972c, p. 80). This 'rapid order' was in stark contrast to programming via punched-card input – where the film-maker was unable to see their output until long after input – with the display, in particular, for Whitney, 'beginning to present new real-time visualizations' (1971b, p. 35).

Describing the first of these experiments, Whitney referred to *Matrix I* (1971) as

> a short film consisting of horizontal and vertical lines, squares and cubes. All motion is along a closed invisible pathway (the matrix) which is a classical Lissajous figure positioned symmetrically within the motion picture field. The motion of the entire film is simply a sequence of events of clustering and dispersal of the lines, squares and cubes.
>
> (1972c, p. 79)

Indeed this visual 'matrix' formed the structural core of all three films, with the motion of composed elements guided within the frame, 'clustering and dispersing', as

Whitney put it, as a multitude of geometric configurations and forms dance in dynamic motion, patterned in close harmony with the musical accompaniment of the piano sonatas of Padre Antonio Soler, in *Matrix I*, and the electronic minimalism of Terry Riley's 'Poppy Nogood and the Phantom Band' (1969, from the album *A Rainbow in Curved Air*), in *Matrix II* (1972) and *Matrix III* (1972), with Riley's multiple layers of saxophone and organ a musical corollary of Whitney's complex, superimposed images.

Geometric forms in *Matrix I* (top) and *Matrix II* and *Matrix III* (bottom; *Matrix II* and *Matrix III* feature the same image track)

Beyond VanDerBeek and Whitney, experiments with computers flourished, not least among Whitney's own family. Son Michael, for instance, produced *Binary Bit Patterns* (1969), an animated film consistent with the aesthetic interests of his father, with the title suitably evocative of the twin concerns of coded expression and abstract composition. Elsewhere, Lillian Schwartz collaborated with Knowlton on films including *Pixillation* (1970) and *Olympiad* (1971) (see Schwartz, 1974, 1976; and with son Laurens, 1992); at Ohio State University, Charles Csuri collaborated with James Shaffer on films such as *Hummingbird* (1967) (see Csuri, 1970; Csuri and Shaffer, 1968); in the computer labs of the University of California, Los Angeles (UCLA), student John Stehura produced *Cibernetik 5.3* (1965–9) (see Youngblood, 1970, pp. 239–46); while, in the UK, the likes of Malcolm Le Grice pursued their own variants, including *Your Lips 1–3* (1970–1) (see Le Grice, 1974, 2001).

Political Protest and the Decline of a Movement

Despite this flurry of 'expanded cinema', and even as Youngblood's influential book of the same name was being published in 1970, wider opinion was split between extremes, with attitudes opposed to the computer and related technology an equally important part of the period's culture concerning computers. Why, we might ask, did this historical moment, and the discourse and expressions it gave rise to, not lead to the sustained paradigm shift envisaged of advanced technology?

For the art and technology movement, as a backdrop to a number of the expressions identified by Youngblood, the collaborations of VanDerBeek and Shaw, VanDerBeek and Knowlton, Whitney and Citron and others, were among the major contributions of cinema to what was ultimately a short-lived movement. While the more general practice of art and technology collaboration continued throughout the 1970s, the momentum and direction of a coherent movement were ultimately lost as attitudes changed. The activities of organisations such as Experiments in Art and Technology and the Art and Technology Program of LACMA gradually dissipated as enthusiasm waned, with the broader notion of a coming together of art and technology as a Utopian gesture, in parallel with the potential of an 'expanded cinema', generally countered by opposition.

On one level, the unbridled faith in technology that characterised much of the discourse of the 1960s – though always in opposition to an equivalent critique of technology – increasingly gave way, by the late 1960s and early 1970s, to a more ambivalent and at times hostile response. Maurice Tuchman, who headed the Art and Technology Program, pointed to a changing sociopolitical climate, which impacted popular perceptions. Writing in October 1970, he speculated:

> I suspect that if Art and Technology were beginning now instead of in 1967, in a climate of increased polarization and organized determination to protest against the policies supported by so many American business interests and so violently opposed by much of the art community, many of the same artists would not have participated.
>
> (1971, p. 17)

At a time of intense political upheaval, major corporations such as IBM functioned as symbols of the established order, emblematic of the military-industrial complex, in particular.

The negative perceptions that Tuchman identified were a response, in large part, to the escalation of conflict in Vietnam. The technological and scientific triumphs of the space race were brutally juxtaposed by the ongoing trauma of the war's painful and protracted close, as beamed around the globe by the recently launched telecommunications satellites and broadcast live on television. Against a backdrop of escalating conflict and a barrage of media coverage, the military-industrial complex and the role of the US Army were central to a significant shift in attitudes concerning advanced technology and the values symbolically associated with it.

Writing in 1973, echoing Tuchman, Douglas Davis framed his study of contemporary art in precise relation to this context of technologised conflict:

> I am more than normally aware that the heady euphoria of the mid-1960s, when artists and engineers came together in significant numbers for the first time, has passed. [...] The war has sickened us all, and we hear little at this hour about the creative potential of technology and much about its destructive capacity.
>
> (1973, p. 11)

For many, the prospect of collaborating with industries so closely aligned with the military, participating in an embrace that would tacitly condone the uses to which these companies' technologies were being put, was seen as anathema.

It was ironic, given the primary role of the US Army in determining the initial development of the digital computer, that it was a changing military context that led to a peak of sentiment in opposition to advanced technology of all kinds. If the computer had emerged – in the form of the ENIAC, first unveiled by J. Presper Eckert and John Mauchly at the University of Pennsylvania, in 1946; a machine designed and manufactured for the purpose of calculating artillery firing tables for the US Army's Ballistics Research Laboratory, though ultimately employed for other purposes (for a history of the ENIAC, see McCartney, 1999) – and proliferated, in the 1940s and 1950s, similarly determined in large part by the investments associated with World War II, the emerging Cold War and the growth of the military-industrial complex, it was the ongoing conflict in Vietnam that caused many to reconsider the role and value of such technology.

It was the military-industrial complex, too – as one constituent of the broader funding stream of the major computer companies – that had provided indirect sponsorship and other opportunities for film-makers and other artists to pursue their aesthetic endeavours in the field of art and technology collaboration. It was in the research and development (R&D) laboratories of institutions such as Bell Labs and IBM, for instance, that the likes of VanDerBeek and Whitney first accessed the technology – now viewed by many with cynicism and suspicion – and associated expertise central to their early experiments with computers, amidst a backdrop of rapid industrial growth.

Articulating this conflict, and the oscillating positions with regard to the technology of the era, even VanDerBeek, who had earlier benefited from his links with Bell Labs, now sought to critique the association of such institutions with the military-industrial complex, and the broader links between technology and war. Formerly one of the most vociferous and at times hyperbolic – in this regard, aligned with Youngblood, and in turn McLuhan and Fuller – advocates of the application of computers to cinema, and to life, VanDerBeek now sought to use these resources to protest against the ongoing conflict in Vietnam.

Poemfield #7 (1971), in particular – produced at Bell Labs, in collaboration with Knowlton, prior to VanDerBeek's work at MIT – reveals the complexity of these attitudes, offering a trace of the continuing conflict. Continuing the 'Poemfields' series of textual abstractions, which used computer processes to transform fragments of poetic text, *Poemfield #7* likewise utilised the computer to pattern and animate verse, commenting on the ongoing war: 'There is no way to peace; peace is the way.' While not protesting technology *per se*, it is nevertheless a revealing coda to a series of films that began in the mid-1960s at the very height of the fervour for art and technology collaboration.

Elsewhere, Knowlton affirmed the increasingly complex relationship with computers – as compared with the techno-Utopianism of Youngblood, for instance – amidst a changing political backdrop. In the year after *Poemfield #7*, he wrote:

> Computers are catching hell from growing multitudes who see them uniformly as the tools of the regulation and suffocation of all things warm, moist, and human. The charges, of course, are not totally unfounded, but in their most sweeping form they are ineffective and therefore actually an acquiescence to the dehumanization which they decry. We clearly need a much more discerning evaluation in order to clarify the ethics of various roles of machines in human affairs.
>
> (1972, p. 399)

Notably, in the midst of this crisis, Knowlton maintained his belief that cinema could continue to offer a way forward, a means of fully understanding the computer, and the world in which it found meaning. Echoing the vision of Youngblood and others, he wrote of how

> One of the most direct – perhaps even brash – ways of doing something about this is to try deliberately to use computers in the production of art – that enterprise which most

> directly seeks to help man to find, experience, and express his humanity, and which seeks to define the good, the true, and the beautiful. The more directly or profoundly a computer usage may be able to touch and extend our human emotions and perceptions, the more, I think, we are likely to perceive it as a possible agent of enhancement rather than one only of restriction.
>
> (1972, p. 399)

Described another way, increasingly powerful computers would continue to offer the possibility of the types of aesthetic and associated expansions envisaged by Youngblood and others.

Conclusion

The experiments of 'expanded cinema', in all its forms, resonated with the radical ideas of McLuhan and Fuller, as visionaries of the digital age, in turn referenced and applied to the moving image by the equally techno-Utopian Youngblood.

The films of VanDerBeek, Whitney and others contributed to a dichotomy of debate concerning technology – extending broader Utopian or technophilic perspectives, on the one hand, and dystopian or technophobic perspectives, on the other – with the evangelical zeal of much of the 1960s giving way to a more ambivalent and at times antagonistic relationship with technology, as initial optimism ebbed against a growing tide of cynicism and political retrenchment. These ideas have been echoed in subsequent decades, but reached particular peaks in the late 1960s and early 1970s in a context of widespread tumult.

In terms of anxieties concerning the computer, and the symbolism and destructive power of advanced technology, more generally, this period represented the art and technology movement's apex, just as related experiments in the use of the computer as a tool for cinema were about to be acknowledged by the commercial film industry.

[7]

To See Ourselves as Androids See Us: The Pixel Perspectives of *Westworld* (1973)

At one point, in Michael Crichton's *Westworld*, the futuristic resort of the film's title is proclaimed as 'the vacation of the future today'. Crichton and others might have made their own lofty claim, that of offering the special effects of the future today, for *Westworld* represents a significant technological landmark in its early adoption of the computer as a tool for graphics. While this technique accounts for only a small percentage of the finished film, this material is nevertheless significant – both to the film's narrative meaning, most obviously, and the broader history of such techniques, in terms of our theorising of technological change.

Specifically, *Westworld* is notable for its use of computer graphics within a commercial context, adopting techniques and aesthetics associated with the experimental cinema of the late 1960s and early 1970s, where computer animation flourished in the years prior to Hollywood finding its own application. Via film-maker John Whitney, Jr, in particular, the high-art, modernist abstraction of 'expanded cinema' (see Youngblood, 1970) was recontextualised and adapted for Crichton's Hollywood 'genre pic', which included Whitney, Jr (credited for his 'automated image processing') on its crew.

In detailing this process, questions of timing come to the fore. For all its innovation, *Westworld* lagged behind a number of key developments, including the emergence of the computer (the era of commercial digital computing, in particular, is generally thought to have begun in the early 1950s); the production of computer films at sites beyond Hollywood (by scientists and experimental film-makers, often in collaboration, in contexts other than the commercial film industry); and the widespread use of computers as cinematic subject matter (as film-makers absorbed the computer as a source of symbolic threat, on the level of story, long before its uses were pioneered, on the level of production).

Considering theories of technological change and the social shaping or construction of technology, why did it take so long for a film such as *Westworld* to be made? What factors, historically specific and otherwise, determined the utilisation of the computer? What does Crichton's film reveal about the changing status of this technology and its roles in Hollywood and the avant-garde? And what might narrative themes and their expression reveal about the broader dynamics of technological change?

Computer Graphics as Special Effect

Westworld's production intertwined the motivations, perspectives and demands of disparate parties, including a film-maker steeped in avant-garde practice (Whitney, Jr), a technology company best known for its digital scanners (Information International, Inc., or III), a debutant Hollywood director (Crichton) and a major Hollywood studio (Metro-Goldwyn-Mayer, or MGM). Not coincidentally, these various interests came together on a film concerned with the computer and its anthropomorphised extension, the android.

In terms of plot, *Westworld* constitutes relatively conventional generic fare, albeit a hybridised conjoining of the science fiction and Western genres. At a futuristic resort, Delos, tourists consume the very latest in robotic fantasies. Three themed venues serve to please and amuse: Romanworld, 'peopled' by subservient androids in appropriate historical garb; Medievalworld, likewise, which features banquets and jousts; and the eponymous Westworld, a recreation of the American frontier, where visitors partake in an orgy of gunfights, saloon brawls and other gratuitous fantasies. Each of these scenarios involves robotic counterparts who are 'scientifically programmed to look, act, talk, and even bleed just like humans do', as one character puts it. Yet,

The computer's remote control of its anthropomorphised extension, the android

Delos becomes a death-trap when its androids – including a deadly gunslinger (played by Yul Brynner) – begin to run amok. Compounding the calamity, the computers relied on to maintain these machines also malfunction, with similarly fatal consequences.

The computer is represented as a technology that mediates between humans and their robotic *doppelgängers*. If the fantasies and fears that go hand in hand with the development of robots that look, act and feel increasingly 'human' are the film's major themes (for an extended discussion of the android's role, see Telotte, 1995, who discusses the ontological confusion – 'a confusion that can be [...] by turns exhilarating and frightening', p. 131 – associated with a machine intelligence increasingly indistinguishable from ourselves; for a discussion of the development of robotics in the historical world, meanwhile, see Raphael, 1976), the computer nevertheless occupies an important role as the tool entrusted with programming an ordered relationship between 'us' and 'them'.

The robotic ontology of *Westworld*'s android run amok (below and opposite)

In the shape of the android, the computer has made the leap towards embodiment, physically rendered not just in the familiar presence of keyboards, displays and other hardware, but in the parallel form of human appearance. This entity is more than a mechanical automaton; rather, it is an extension of the computers that drive it, representing a physical manifestation of this technology. Accordingly, we assess the actions of *Westworld*'s androids in parallel with their underlying programming.

In searching for a cinematic style and technique to signify this hybrid subjectivity – ostensibly human, inherently machine – the film-makers faced a difficult proposition. As Whitney, Jr described it, writing in *American Cinematographer*, the problem posed was 'to find a technique to represent, on film, the point of view of a machine [... and] for the audience to see the world as a robot gunfighter [...] saw it' (1973, p. 1478).

Crichton, for his part, recalled how traditional techniques fell short of representing a distinctly digital perspective. In the film's published screenplay, he described how his team 'reviewed standard special-effects techniques and rejected them all; they were too familiar, and shared a "filmic" quality – no matter how strange, they still looked like photographic images. I didn't want that' (1974, p. xii).

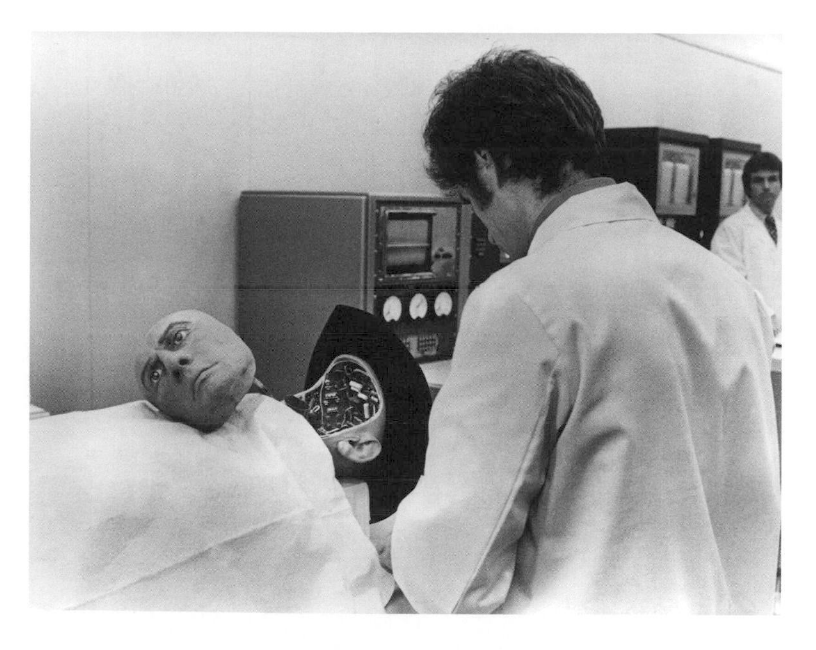

Instead, a fundamental corollary was proposed between the digital subjectivity of the android gunslinger, on the one hand, and the means of producing the computer graphics that would signify its robotic ontology, on the other. As Crichton put it, the proposal was 'the idea that the machine world-view would be literally that – a series of pictures created by computer' (1974, p. xii), a notion affirmed by Whitney, Jr's recollection that 'key to the project was the unheard of idea of processing several scenes for the movie' (2007) – 'processing' meaning the computer manipulation of existing footage.

Form and content would be matched through an innovative digital scanning technique, which would create a pixellated visual effect for those shots from the gunslinger's point of view. 'I knew it was possible to scan images with a computer, and then reconstitute those images in some other form', Crichton continued. 'I didn't know whether these techniques could be applied to motion picture film, but the idea seemed worth exploring' (1974, p. xii).

While this particular technique had yet to be incorporated within a Hollywood feature – 'Several experts told us that this was impossible' (1974, p. xii), Crichton explained – similar techniques were not unheard of outside Hollywood. In particular, the likes of avant-garde luminary John Whitney – father of Whitney, Jr – had pioneered the computer's function as a tool for animation, with abstract graphics generated – frame by frame – in pursuit of a mode of expressive, experimental cinema quite distinct from the norms of Hollywood.

In bridging these contexts, Whitney, Jr personified a broader industrial evolution. In the approximately two minutes of Crichton's film produced using computers –

consisting of close to 3,000 separate images across fourteen sequences – Whitney, Jr adapted a series of techniques originally developed outside the commercial film industry. This shift – from a mode of experimental film-making to a role at the very core of a Hollywood film – paralleled the computer's changing status, more generally.

Prior to *Westworld*, Whitney, Jr had worked independently employing the analogue, mechanical computers pioneered by his father. Films such as *Byjina Flores* (1964) – in which, in Gene Youngblood's words, 'filamented, fluted panels of neon-bright red, orange, and yellow shift rhythmically across the range of vision to produce weird perspectival illusions and kinetic trajectories' (1970, p. 230) – extended the Whitney family tradition of abstract film-making, in contrast to the narrative context of *Westworld*.

More complexly, a second film, *Terminal Self* (1971) – again, produced with analogue computers – is more nuanced in its relationship between abstract and figurative concerns, anticipating the aesthetic and technical approach adopted in *Westworld*. In *Terminal Self*, an image of a woman's face gradually abstracts and fragments, dissolving into countless coloured multiples, before slowly reforming as a single image – a process of deconstructing an otherwise representational image that prefigures the pixellation of *Westworld*.

Abstract as well as figurative concerns in *Terminal Self*

It was at III – where the elder Whitney had worked with computers in the early 1970s – that Whitney, Jr further developed these practices, shaping his aesthetic concerns in relation to the specific needs of Crichton and MGM. For Gary Demos – who worked with Whitney, Jr at III from 1974 as part of the Motion Pictures Product Group – this company, founded in 1962, 'was the world leader in digital film scanning and recording technology for microfilms' (2005, p. 963). Its core business of producing digital scanners was well suited to the particular imaging demands of *Westworld*.

In developing this application, Whitney, Jr reimagined technology intended for one context by redeploying it in another. This creative strategy extended an approach developed by his father, whose earliest computer films were produced on surplus mechanical equipment discarded by the military. In Whitney, Jr's case, this was equipment, he explained, 'that was not actually made for motion-picture work [...], but could be made to work, along with the writing of the code, to create the "look"' (2007) – a description that might equally describe the gunslinger's optical perspective and the visual aesthetic associated with it.

As well as computers, equipment assembled at III included, according to Whitney, Jr, 'A scanner and recorder with non-pin-registered 35mm film transports' (2007). Collectively, these devices were used for scanning images into the computer, where they could be manipulated with dedicated software, before being exported as film.

Pixellation was a central element of this scanning system, with footage shot by traditional means in turn digitised and visually marked as such as a way of signifying the gunslinger's subjectivity. Whitney, Jr explained how 'an image is broken down into a series of points, and the grey-scale value for each point determined. A numerical value can then be assigned to each point, and a new image reconstituted electronically' (1973, p. 1478). Working one frame at a time, Whitney, Jr divided each image into a grid of small squares (3,600 per anamorphic frame of film), sampling their various hues and intensity of light before averaging each as a single colour – a process repeated for every square of every image.

In scanning 35mm film for computer manipulation, an analogue source was converted into digital data – the zeros and ones of binary code. In this form, the footage was rendered especially malleable, prone to creative manipulation, a state that Lev Manovich describes – in outlining the 'principles of new media' (2001, pp. 27–48) – in terms of 'numerical representation' (2001, pp. 27–30), by which a media object is 'subject to algorithmic manipulation [...] *programmable*' (2001, p. 27).

Such 'algorithmic manipulation' was key to the pixellated shots of *Westworld*, in which conventionally filmed footage, when converted into numerical code, was transformed through programmed equations. As Whitney, Jr explained:

> Once the computer has 'read' the image and converted it to a series of numbers, there is tremendous flexibility in what the computer can then do with this numerical information. The image can be reconstituted with different contrasts, different resolutions, different colors. We can enlarge, stretch, squeeze, twist, rotate it, position it in space in any way. In

> fact, the only limitations are imposed by the creative talents of the person operating the machine.
>
> (1973, p. 1478)

Under Whitney, Jr's operation, dedicated programming controlled precise instructions for how images were scanned, digitised and manipulated.

The result was the creation of a series of mosaics or quantised patterns. Each, in composite, depicts figures and landscapes algorithmically processed to convey the optical perspective of a digital entity. In motion, meanwhile, successive images shimmer according to the play of pixellation as the thousands of squares per image change colour, flickering between digitally scanned tones.

By reworking recognisable landscapes and objects according to a representational corollary of the pixel, *Westworld* utilised the computer as a formal reflection of the thematic investigation of android subjectivity, the anthropomorphised manifestation of a simulated world controlled by computers in one form or another. On both

The gaze of the android gunslinger

literal and symbolic levels, the grain of film was transformed into a visual texture synonymous with the computer, with the Western's iconography reworked through the process of pixellation. As the androids embark on their murderous spree, it is through Whitney, Jr's special effect that we glimpse an insight into the film's technological foe.

Questions of Determinism

'A new device merely opens a door', Lynn White, Jr has written, identifying the social factors that shape the development and reception of technology, 'it does not compel one to enter' (1962, p. 28). What factors, we might ask, compelled Crichton and MGM to enter the 'door' opened by the computer's commercial availability and pushed further ajar by the experimentation of Whitney, Jr and others? Theories of technological change look beyond technology in purely physical terms to consider the demands and uses that shape, direct and even anticipate its invention and utilisation. Applied to *Westworld*, such theories shed light on the timing and nature of this process, revealing the complex interplay of determinants at work in the computer's adoption.

As one example, while acknowledging the importance of Whitney, Jr, it is also necessary to contextualise the role of individuals, to consider the institutions and cultural settings in which they exist. As David Bordwell and Kristin Thompson argue, 'While technological and artistic innovations can usually be attributed to individuals, those individuals operate within a broader context' (1993, p. 119). Without accounting for this 'broader context', an emphasis on the role of individuals risks falling foul of what Douglas Gomery terms the 'great man' theory (1985a), whereby 'so long as one holds that the ultimate "cause" of technological change is the genius of a few individuals, then there is not much else in the way of historical explanation that need be said' (1985a, p. 111; for a further debunking of this tendency, see Winston, 1996, pp. 10–38).

In accordance with such 'historical explanation', it is equally necessary to extend beyond a straightforward notion that computers were simply not powerful enough until 1973 – the year of *Westworld* – at which point certain technological constraints were overcome. While it is clear that the computers of the early 1970s were rudimentary by today's standards, it is also the case that many outside Hollywood – whether scientists, experimental film-makers or both in collaboration – had been making films with the aid of computers for a decade or more before *Westworld*.

Just as important as the technical parameters of technology, for Steve Neale, typical of those theorists concerned with questions of determinism, are 'Aesthetic, economic, legal or political facts and factors' (1985, p. 159), among other determinants. The interplay of these 'facts and factors' supplant a more general faith in the relentless, autonomous drive of technological evolution, and help explain why the computer's emergence did not immediately translate into the film industry, despite the proliferating uses of this technology in other sectors and fields.

Notably, juxtaposing the often Utopian and countercultural attitudes and philosophy of 'expanded cinema', the application of computers to *Westworld* represented a utilisation within the explicitly commercial context of Hollywood. Here, according to Bordwell and Thompson, 'a systematic approach to technological innovation and assimilation' (1993, p. 141) had operated for many decades and continues to operate. Described another way, *Westworld*'s producers identified a potential utility – what is typically referred to as a 'use-value' (see Marx, 1887 [originally 1867]), in terms of political economy, or as part of the processes of 'closure' and 'stabilization' (1995), in the models of the social construction of technology outlined by Wiebe Bijker. What these concepts share is an awareness of the social reception of technology and the importance of the perception of possible uses and commercial applications.

For Bijker, in particular, there is a dual process by which any new technology – which might exist in many different forms, performing many different functions – assumes the 'closure' of a particular or dominant meaning, first, before additional meanings are arrived at in specific contexts, second, through the process of 'stabilization'.

Of the initial stage, Bijker explains, 'closure' describes 'the process by which interpretative flexibility decreases, leaving the meanings attributed to the artifact less and less ambiguous' (1995, pp. 270–1). The forms and functions of the technology in question become more and more fixed, as with the increasingly dominant understanding of the computer as a 'universal machine' (Turing, 1936), one with widespread applications beyond the military-industrial complex.

The related notion of 'stabilization' refers to the uses and meanings ascribed to a given technology by a specific group within society – in this instance, Hollywood, as represented by Crichton and MGM. Where the concept of 'closure' emphasises shared meanings, 'stabilization' refers, as Bijker notes, to 'the development of the artifact itself within one relevant social group, in terms of the modalities used in its descriptions' (1995, p. 87). With the computer as 'artifact', we might point to *Westworld* as emblematic of the determinants of how the computer – already pioneered in the context of experimental cinema, as one example – was exploited within Hollywood's distinctive 'mode of production' (Bordwell *et al.*, 1985). Factors specific to the commercial film industry, in other words, determined – at least, in part

– the extended period between 'closure' and 'stabilization', with utilisation, in this context, occurring long after purely technological preconditions had been met.

For Bijker, a staggered response to new technology is not unusual. 'The combination of stabilization and closure processes makes it understandable that technical change is a continuous process', he explains, 'although not one that occurs at equal rates at every point in time; it is more like a punctuated evolution' (1995, pp. 87–8). Where the general shape of a technology reaches widespread consensus, its specific applications within individual sectors often vary, determined at quite different times.

For Karl Marx, the 'use-value' of any labour product, whether an object or service, is determined by its capacity to satisfy a particular need or want in society. The 'use-value' of the computer, for instance, or of the knowledge, skills, or services associated with this technology, was determined not by a producer – in this instance, by the manufacturers of the devices engaged in Whitney, Jr's scanning process – but by those in the wider world who perceived its uses and values. For technology to be exchanged and commodified, a 'use-value' must be perceived and determined by the broader market, at which point its 'use-value' becomes a 'social use-value' (Marx, 1887).

Writing in *Capital*, Marx explains the relationship between a 'use-value' and its subsequent commodification. 'The utility of a thing makes it a use-value' (1887, p. 2), he notes, defining this notion in terms of the perceived benefit or profitable application of the 'thing' in question:

> A thing can be useful, and the product of human labour, without being a commodity. Whoever directly satisfies his wants with the produce of his own labour, creates, indeed, use-values, but not commodities. In order to produce the latter, he must not only produce use-values, but use-values for others, social use-values.
>
> (1887, pp. 7–8)

In short, a value must be perceived beyond the producer for a 'thing' to be rendered commercial.

While Marx was little concerned with the specificity of technology, and not at all with the systematic evolution of the technologies of cinema – necessarily, given the time of writing, which predates the generally accepted 'birth' of cinema in 1895 – his ideas nevertheless provide a useful model for thinking about the commodification of technology within the broader workings of capital. In relation to *Westworld*, the economic viability of integrating the computer would likely have played a major role in determining the possibilities open to Crichton, and the arrival at an application – and 'use-value' – consistent with commercial imperatives.

For others, too, in terms of cinema, the timing and nature of technological change can be understood in terms of industrial and economic determinants. According to Gomery, 'as the American cinema took on the characteristics of a mature capitalist industry – that is to say, a collection of firms, each trying to generate maximum long-run profits – technological change became largely a matter of economic decision making' (1985a, p. 114; for particular applications in the context of the coming of sound, see 1985b, 2005). Technological change, in other words, is intimately bound up in the range of business strategies intrinsic to industrial production. In the instance of *Westworld*, we might consider the diminishing costs of computers and associated expertise. The impact of rapid acceleration – described by 'Moore's law' (Moore, 1965), which quantifies the exponential increase in the number of components on an integrated circuit in relation to their minimum cost; an equation symbolic of a wider technological acceleration – in the relative performance of computers, as one example, would likely have significantly determined the commercial appeal (or otherwise) of this technology for Hollywood.

In related industrial and institutional terms, the emergence and growth of a computer graphics industry – with its specialist knowledge and skills increasingly available in a commercial market – opened up the very possibility of MGM working with a company such as III. By 1973, the computer graphics industry had developed to such an extent that a studio like MGM, which had yet to produce its own digital effects, could commission a dedicated company. The firm III typified this burgeoning field, and was well equipped, given the expertise and experience of Whitney, Jr, in particular, to respond to the commercial potential of computer graphics in the context of Hollywood.

Elsewhere, an additional material factor was the marketing potential associated with the computer as a 'new' technology. 'Since at least 1930, Hollywood has promoted mechanical marvels as assiduously as it has publicized stars, properties, and genres' (1985, p. 243), write Bordwell and Janet Staiger, outlining the 'novelties' (1985, p. 243) and 'product differentiation' (1985, p. 244) associated with technological change. In this context, the use of computers was as much a marketing strategy as it was an exclusively technological innovation.

In general, the broad assumption is that companies and corporations – in this instance, MGM – will always act in ways designed to maximise profits, with technological change carefully managed and exploited for commercial gain, with the example of the computer no exception to the general rule.

Yet, the interplay of industrial and economic factors cannot be entirely understood by a straightforward notion of affordability and profitability. Such ideas are complicated by the creative practices associated with the broader economic framework of Hollywood. To reprise and extend White, Jr, it is not just the entering of an opened door that is significant, but precisely how it is entered. Applied to the realm of cinema, via *Westworld*, questions of genre, style and narrative – as they exist in an industrial, classical paradigm – are equally key to our understanding of technological change.

Classical Hollywood Cinema

The use of computers in a Hollywood feature film is quite different from the context of experimental cinema, with these differences intimately related to institutional and other factors, registered on the level of narrative – or its absence. Issues of style, for instance, are equally key to the timing and nature of technological change. In Hollywood, the classical paradigm – and its rules, norms or conventions – is a primary determinant of this process. In relation to *Westworld*, techniques and aesthetics pioneered outside Hollywood were adopted in accordance with this classical paradigm.

In theorising this context, Bordwell, Staiger and Thompson have done much to nuance the debate concerning the industrial and economic dimensions of technological change, to also consider style as a key determinant and marker of this process. 'As might be expected', write Bordwell and Thompson in outlining this dynamic, 'technology often creates new devices or reinforces or revises existing ones' (1993, p. 109). Where Bordwell and Staiger highlight the evolutionary developments of sound, colour, widescreen and stereophonic sound (1985), we might add to their list the 'new devices' associated with computer graphics.

In terms of a prevailing, determining framework, Bordwell, Staiger and Thompson point to the ways in which technological change in Hollywood is typically linked to the distinctive mode of film-making associated with this context. On a local level, for instance, 'Film-makers' beliefs about proper film technique make certain kinds of change more acceptable than others' (Bordwell and Thompson, 1993, p. 109). More broadly and systematically, they continue, 'technology is itself guided by both the characteristic devices and broader goals' (1993, p. 109) of Hollywood style.

Specifically, they describe the process of technological change as one carefully managed so as not to rupture the stylistic status quo. New technology, they argue, fulfils an industrial function carefully managed to augment, but not undermine – 'product differentiation must not destroy stylistic standardization' (Bordwell and Staiger,

1985, p. 245) – the existing aesthetic paradigm, with a major aim being 'maximal integration with, or extension of, the classical stylistic norms' (Bordwell and Thompson, 1993, p. 116).

Brian Winston, likewise, has written of the suppression of radical potential, with several industrial benefits associated with delaying or staggering the adoption of new technology. In Winston's model, 'Constraints operate to slow the rate of diffusion so that the social fabric in general can absorb the new machine and essential formations such as business entities and other institutions can be protected and preserved' (1998, p. 11). The implication, applied to the context of Hollywood and the computer in the years before *Westworld*, is that the more radical the potential for new aesthetics – fundamental to the techno-Utopian agenda of 'expanded cinema', for example – the more deliberately constrained the rate of diffusion, in Hollywood, in order that the status quo be 'protected and preserved'.

The 'stylistic standardization' referred to by Bordwell and Staiger, key to the 'essential formations' described by Winston, is best understood in terms of the umbrella term 'classical Hollywood cinema' (see Bordwell *et al.*, 1985), to which *Westworld* broadly belongs, albeit just beyond the cusp of the transition from classical to post-classical cinematic style (which Bordwell *et al.*, 1985, ascribe to the end of the 1950s and the beginning of the 1960s). This notion describes a set of institutions, and associated mode of film production, distinctive to Hollywood. While neither universal nor monolithic, a set of stylistic norms, conventions and principles, designed to serve the primacy of narrative and its communication, have nevertheless endured over a number of decades.

So-called 'invisible' style, for example, described as such because it does not call attention to itself as even being a style, encourages the viewer to stay emotionally involved in a film's story and characters, as opposed to being 'distracted' by formal or stylistic devices, including reflexive markers of the technological means of production – though the spectacular appeal associated with special effects, in particular, complicate this broader rule (for a discussion of the relationship between narrative and spectacle in the context of special effects, see McClean, 2007).

In *Westworld*, conforming to classical norms, computer graphics are seamlessly integrated, rendered 'invisible' – introduced, in other words, according to the conventions of classical narration, whereby style is necessarily subordinate to narrative demands. Computer graphics are given a narrative context, part of a systematic combination of thematics, technology and technique.

In generic terms, meanwhile, the flirtation with science fiction – populated, as a staple, by high-tech themes and associated special effects – offers a degree of

Optical point of view in *Lady in the Lake*

verisimilitude for the introduction of computer graphics. If the computer's characteristic visual signature, in 1973, was largely unsuitable for narrative realism, the process of pixellation found ample motivation in the generic conventions of science fiction.

The function of point of view in the film's pixellated footage offers useful illustration of the narrative – and, in turn, generic – anchoring of computer graphics. Beyond Whitney, Jr's innovation, the underlying narrative conventions associated with the point-of-view shot (for a general history, see Branigan, 1984) – pixellated or otherwise – are well established, typically conservative. Indeed the point-of-view shot dates back to early cinema, and arguably reached its formal apex more than a quarter of a century before *Westworld*, in Robert Montgomery's *Lady in the Lake* (1946), a film constructed almost entirely from a succession of such shots. This is not to preclude the possibility of radical or experimental applications, but to suggest, in this instance, the augmentation, rather than rupturing, of the existing paradigm.

In this respect, it is also notable that the strand of aesthetic abstraction central to the likes of the elder Whitney, and similarly present in the early computer films of

Whitney, Jr, is recontextualised in *Westworld* according to figurative and representational concerns, creating a peculiar fusion. The shots that convey the gunslinger's optical perspective depict figures and landscapes at once both recognisable – specifically, as elements of the Western's *mise en scène* – and partly abstracted, made strange through the process of computerised visualisation. In one example, we see a generically archetypal rock formation, replete with rich cinematic associations suggestive of John Ford and others, except that here the image is rendered alien, decidedly digital.

That abstraction does not exist in *Westworld* in its purest sense, as it did in the precursors of 'expanded cinema' – where abstraction was viewed as an end in its own right, with the aim of stimulating the eye (and, by extension, the other senses too) – and is instead motivated by narrative signification, is consistent with the computer's recontextualisation to a classical paradigm, where the support for realism was and remains a fundament or ideal of the prevailing aesthetic regime. The impulse towards abstraction, characteristic of many of the computer films produced in the late 1960s and early 1970s, gives way in *Westworld* to a technologised variation on the more familiar trope of photorealism. Whitney, Jr's computer graphics are subject to the control of a repressive narrative logic, lest pixellation reflexively rupture 'invisible' style or disrupt narrative momentum.

Such 'stylistic standardization', to reprise Bordwell and Staiger, is in stark contrast to the determined differentiation of 'expanded cinema', which sought an altogether new representational mode or aesthetic, the quintessence of the computer and the age that gave rise to its proliferation.

That the use of this technology in *Westworld* was motivated by narrative concerns is consistent with the norms of Hollywood. If computer graphics could only assume a role in the commercial film industry so long as they could operate effectively within the parameters of classical practices, at the service of efficient narration, then the efforts of Whitney, Jr and others went some way to achieving this. Aligning the aesthetic experimentation of the 1960s with its commercial potential in the 1970s, *Westworld* represented a model of computer graphics more fully integrated with the narrative and other demands of Hollywood.

Conclusion

Via whichever or all – and probably others besides – of the various factors and determinants discussed in this chapter, *Westworld* is notable for its early uses of the computer. In addition to its role on the level of story – where *Westworld* can be read as a morality tale, an inversion of the master–slave relationship with regard to technological invention, whereby human progenitors are punished by the very machines they unleash – Crichton's film is significant, in the history of cinema, for ushering this technology, and computer graphics, into the realm of the commercial film industry.

The precise timing and extended period between the emergence of this technology and its subsequent adoption are consistent with various precedents and precursors, as well as theoretical models of technological change. The film's use of computer graphics conforms to the norms of Hollywood, both on the level of institutional economics – where technological change is managed and in turn exploited according to commercial considerations – and how these broader systems feed into, and are manifested in, related conventions concerning the narrative function of new technology, particularly in terms of the role of special effects.

In its historically specific conjuncture of myriad determinants, *Westworld* evidenced the arrival of an industrially perceived 'use-value', to quote Marx, or a process of 'stabilization', in the words of Bijker. This is not to say that every Hollywood film would immediately follow *Westworld*'s lead, or that the computer animations and other abstract, experimental forms that preceded it would instantly cease to exist – far from it. Rather, a symbolic juncture had been reached. For Crichton and MGM, illustrative of the commercial film industry, the computer had assumed a utility that would contribute – via its stylistically regulated narrative function – to profitability.

Films such as *Westworld* would increasingly become the norm, with the computer an ever more central tool. While it would take several more years for this technology to be fully absorbed within the cinematic apparatus, Crichton's film established a precedent for this continued integration. In doing so, it signalled the end of one history, or prehistory – the various films and film-makers explored in this book – and the start of another, far more recognisable and familiar, which would begin rather than end with the technological feat of *Westworld*.

Conclusion

> The future of the past is in the future
> The future of the present is in the past
> The future of the future is in the present.
>
> John McHale (1969, unpaginated frontispiece)

Looking beyond the dawn of the digital age, it is important to consider what this era anticipated; that is, what seeds – symbolic, aesthetic and so on – were sown, and have subsequently flourished, in terms of the relationship between cinema and computers. As McHale's gnomic, cryptic comment suggests, the fields of past, present and future are intimately bound together by a matrix of intersecting trajectories of influence and insight. Many of the shifts, tendencies and processes detailed in the course of this study have continued to evolve, renegotiated by the shifting patterns of connections across the films and film-makers that followed.

The possibility that this earlier period might be considered in autonomous terms, as opposed to simply as a precursor to what followed, should not be precluded – an equivalent, in this respect, of the critique of early cinema as 'primitive', a notion that Tom Gunning has argued (see 1986, 1989, for example) to be problematic in its retrospective construction as the inevitable, developmental precursor to what Noël Burch has termed the Institutional Mode of Representation (IMR) (1990) of classical, narrative, Hollywood cinema. Yet, this period is interesting, in many respects, precisely because it represents the early stages of an extended period of shift, anticipating or prefiguring trends that have come to the fore in subsequent decades.

Having charted a set of historical contours and argued their coherence, it is also useful to evaluate the importance of what came next. In what ways, we might ask, did cinema's early engagement with computers envisage a later era in which this technology would become ubiquitous in many parts of the world? How has it happened that the computer has become so integral to cinema, in particular? What can we learn, in this context, from those who first pioneered this technology as a cinematic tool? And what, ultimately, is the legacy of this period and its continuing revelations?

Cinema and 'Computer Lib'

In certain respects, expanding our historical purview, the post-war era might be seen as an early glimpse – or even a starting point – of cinema's ultimate 'remediation' (1999), a term coined by Jay David Bolter and Richard Grusin to refer to the processes by which one medium is transformed into another, particularly as a digital variant. To a certain extent, we witness a transition from analogue to digital technology, cinema to digital variants, traditional media to so-called 'new' media, as cinema responded to a machine that it would both absorb and be absorbed by (for a discussion of the supposed 'death of cinema', see Rodowick, 2007, as one example of a contemporary strain of theory that seeks to address the question, 'What *was* cinema?').

'How does computerization affect our very concept of moving images?', Lev Manovich has asked, attempting to ascertain the connections that exist between the distinctive modes of communication associated with cinema, on the one hand, and computing, on the other. 'Does it offer new possibilities for film language? Has it led to the development of totally new forms of cinema?' (2001, p. 287). At the heart of these questions lies the implication that 'new' media function according to a particular set of principles that continue to impact on cinema amidst the contemporary confluence of 'old' and 'new' media referred to by Manovich, but which were first encountered much earlier – as Manovich himself helpfully maps, albeit via a very different path to that of this particular cartography.

While *Westworld* represented a move, in the context of Hollywood, towards the computer's industrial acceptance – consistent with a general pattern of experimentation followed by the adoption of practices and techniques by the cultural mainstream – it is not the case that *Westworld*, in particular, or in isolation, fulfilled this process. Rather, it symbolised the historically specific intersection of a number of developments that collectively marked a shift towards the computer's absorption within the commercial film industry, a process – accretive, gradual, extended – that would take several more years to occur in full, and arguably continues today.

To hint at the fluidity of historical borders, in terms of what came after (and, by implication, before), also reveals and acknowledges the problem of choosing *any* beginning or end point to a historical study. While the scope of this particular framing ostensibly ends in the 1970s – for one must end somewhere – this delineation is not intended to suggest an absolute demarcation, and there is necessarily some overlap, not least in the suggestion that many of the movements and expressions explored would continue, in certain respects, beyond the period under consideration.

After *Westworld*, for example, one can point to the continued growth of computer graphics and special effects. The particular trajectory represented by *Westworld*, with the computer engaged as a production tool by a major Hollywood studio, MGM, would continue in the years after 1973. Instances of films that have featured such graphics, in one form or another, are countless – and include Richard Heffron's *Futureworld* (1976), the sequel to *Westworld*, and Steven Lisberger's *Tron* (1982), as two relatively early examples, both of which feature the special effects of John Whitney, Jr, through Information International, Inc. (III), where he also worked on *Westworld*.

By 1982, for example, less than a decade after Crichton's film, III was one of four companies – which also included MAGI (Mathematical Applications Group, Inc.), Robert Abel and Associates and Digital Effects (see Schrage, 1982) – who would collectively produce the special effects for *Tron*, depicting the type of technological topography associated with the virtual realm described by William Gibson as 'cyberspace' (1984). Notably, if *Tron* offered a significant symbolic departure, depicting not the external architecture of the computer, nor its anthropomorphised extension – the android – but a metaphorical representation of the internal or virtual space of the computer, Gibson's 'cyberspace', it also extended the technological processes represented by *Westworld*. In this sense, it demonstrates the dramatic growth of computer graphics, in relation to Hollywood, and the increasing number of companies with the specialist technology and expertise to work on such techniques, in terms of the links between industries, to the point where such effects are now a fundamental part of much of cinema (see McClean, 2007; Pierson, 2002).

'Cyberspace' and the computer graphics of *Tron*

This is not to say that an avant-garde tradition of abstract computer animation ceased to exist, or that there was an immediate end to the work of film-makers in institutions outside Hollywood. In the 1970s and beyond, continuing the practices established in the 1960s, in terms of digital computers, and even earlier, in terms of analogue antecedents, pioneers such as John Whitney and Stan VanDerBeek continued to create films, maintaining their exploration of the interface between cinema and computers, though now divorced from the context of the organised art and technology movement that had flourished in previous years.

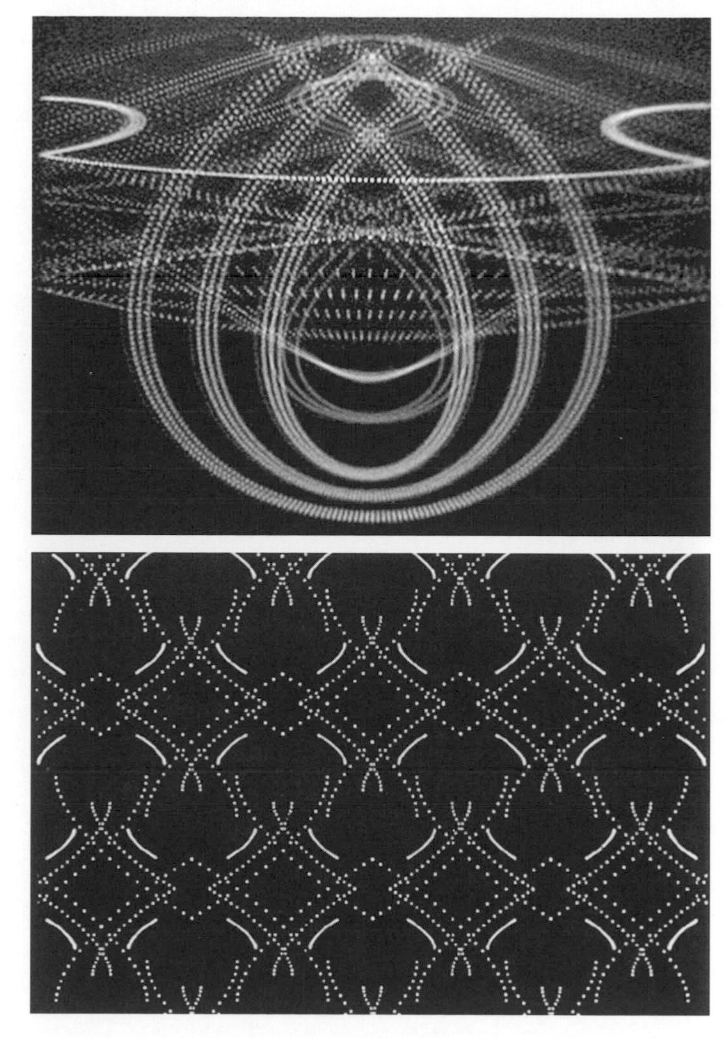

Arabesque (top), *Two Space* (bottom) and the succession of art and technology

For Whitney, as one example, later works sought to build on the initial pursuit of an abstract cinema produced in collaboration with research laboratories, computer companies and specialist employees. *Arabesque* (1975), for instance, was produced at III with software programmed by Larry Cuba, reprising the types of relationships forged at IBM in the 1960s. Inspired by Islamic geometric forms and calligraphy, *Arabesque* represents a degree of continuity with Whitney's creative concerns, with abstract visuals composed in motion. VanDerBeek, likewise, would continue to pursue his experiments with cinema and the expanded consciousness associated with new technology, and even worked in collaboration with NASA at the end of the 1970s (see Claus, 2003).

Following in the footsteps of this first generation of pioneers of abstract computer animation were others – including Cuba (in films such as *Two Space* [1979] and *Calculated Movements* [1985]), separate from his work with Whitney – who sought to extend the commitment to an experimental cinema. The likes of Cuba continued to pursue the creative possibilities envisaged by Whitney, VanDerBeek and others, but did so in relative isolation, as the period of burgeoning discourse and culture of collaboration that characterised the 1960s art and technology movement steadily declined.

The particular need for collaboration, evidenced most markedly in the 1960s, gradually dissipated – absorbed within the dominant culture, on the one hand, and obviated by the increasing availability of consumer technology, on the other. The model of an intimate pairing between artist and technologist, which had been an important feature of the computer's creative genesis in the 1960s and early 1970s, and which played an important part in facilitating access for film-makers, gradually became redundant. Collaboration between film-makers and programmers still existed – and exists today, of course – but in far less explicit or collectively organised ways.

In terms of a changing culture, more generally, the search for a new conception of the computer – represented, on one level, by the art and technology movement, in terms of the perspectives and motivations of those involved in collaboration, and the corporations and industries that sponsored exchange – anticipated increasing access to computers across all sectors of society and a heightened sense of the universality of this machine in terms of the tasks it might perform.

If computers in the 1950s were primarily confined to major laboratories and their clients (in terms of the prohibitive cost of access), limited to the specific agendas and niche applications of these institutions (in terms of expected functions), and restricted to the specialist skills of scientists, technicians and engineers (in terms of the knowledge required to fully understand their workings), then by the 1970s, as the expressions of film-makers and other artists illustrate, such machines were increasingly recognised as tools that might perform a variety of functions, with uses and users beyond those typically associated with more established and familiar sectors. Out of the search for new conceptions came a diversification away from the computer as the exclusive preserve of specialists, towards greater access for film-makers and other artists, as proxies for the wider population.

'Ready or not, computers are coming to the people', wrote Stewart Brand in *Rolling Stone*. 'That's good news, maybe the best since psychedelics' (1972, p. 33). The uses of the computer as a cinematic tool – one that might manifest the previously unseen in the pursuit of distinctively digital expressions – formed the vanguard for the type of 'computer lib' (1974, pp. 1–69) envisaged by Ted Nelson, whereby technology would be freed from elite engineers and from institutionally prescribed applications.

Advances in technology, alongside shifts in popular perceptions, opened up the possibility of the computer becoming a tool that might be used far and wide, in all manner of applications. As part of this movement towards democratisation, cinema helped pave the way – or at least offered a precedent – for the computer's expressive potential.

'Computer lib' would accelerate in the form of the personal computers, or 'dream machines' (Nelson, 1974, pp. DM1–DM59), of the 1970s and beyond, following the mainframes, minicomputers and microcomputers of the post war decades. The launch of the personal computer, with the unveiling of the MITS (Micro Instrumentation Telemetry Systems) Altair 8800, in 1974, and the subsequent development of personal appliances by IBM, Apple and others, would further impact on the computer's price, size and accessibility, with the notion of personal interaction an important part of the evolution of creative applications. The significant barriers between film-makers and computers that Whitney, VanDerBeek and others had striven so earnestly to overcome would erode still further to the point of near disappearance, in terms of creative vision and its intuitive expression via tools that are accessible, inexpensive and technically straightforward.

The 'dream machine' challenged popular notions of what computers were for. After all, exhorted Nelson, 'computer lib' would enable and facilitate a range of applications – including, by implication, in the realm of cinema – limited only by the imagination, as he outlined a belief that the importance of computers lay not in existing applications, but in giving rise to new forms. 'People have legitimate complaints about the way computers are used, and legitimate ideas for ways they should be used, which should no longer be shunted aside' (1974, p. 2), he argued. Such writing was an attempt to destabilise the existing order of the computer industry, and the broader culture concerning computers, so as to encourage the conceptualisation of a truly liberatory tool.

In this sense, Nelson's writing was also an attempt to debunk the idea of the computer as a cold, sterile, *im*personal machine – a perception to which many of the films of the preceding years had contributed. Extending broader technophobic perspectives, films such as *Desk Set*, *Alphaville*, *2001: A Space Odyssey* and *Westworld* had established, in relation to the computer, the symbolic norm by which, as T. J. Matheson has described, 'Among films that are explicitly concerned with society's relationship to the technological milieu, any celebrations of technology have been far outnumbered by films that present it as having had a negative effect on the quality of human life' (1992, p. 326). Offering cautionary tales whose genesis was rooted in society's fears, cinema framed the computer as a source of significant threat, potentially destructive and dehumanising – the very opposite of 'computer lib'.

Nevertheless, although the computer of the 1970s was not yet a 'dream machine', in Nelson's terms, many of the precedents for future developments in computing had already been established, reflected in the moving image. In terms of fundamental architecture, for instance, if the computer had emerged as a specialist, sequential, batch processor of symbols – that is, as a machine for storing, retrieving and processing information – it evolved into an increasingly real-time, graphical, intelligent, interactive machine, characteristics that are staples of today's computing. In short, the computer of the 1970s represented a very different technology to the one first projected in films such as *Desk Set*.

The shift from batch processing to real-time operation, for instance, evidenced increasingly towards the end of this period, and a central element of the discourse concerning experiments in cinema, anticipated the type of immediacy in computing that has since become the norm. In terms of operation, almost all of the computers of the 1950s, including the machine depicted in *Desk Set*, were sequential batch processors, dedicated to performing a single task at a time. The high cost of hardware, in particular, made it impractical for users to interact with their machines. Alternatively, programs were submitted by multiple users on decks of punched cards, well in advance of their actual computation. The computer would then perform its calculations as a 'batch' before outputting its data, typically through a paper printout. Needless to say, this was a technology far from conducive to the production of moving images. Yet, by the end of this period, there was a shift away from batch processing towards real-time operation, whereby the computer would respond virtually instantaneously to continuous input.

Likewise, in terms of the computer as a machine for graphics – necessarily essential for cinema – a number of experiments pioneered this potential. The computer was transformed, in its employment across a number of military and scientific contexts, and in its application to the output of moving images – from the scientific visualisations at Bell Labs and the animations of Whitney, VanDerBeek and others to the computer-generated imagery (CGI) of Whitney, Jr. The computer evolved as a machine capable of sophisticated graphics, anticipating the growing role of CGI and related special effects.

At the same time, progress was also achieved – as articulated by the moving image, from *Alphaville* to *2001: A Space Odyssey* – in the more speculative realm of artificial intelligence. The computer was increasingly seen as a machine that might be programmed to demonstrate, or at least simulate, the ability to acquire and apply knowledge and learning. Advances in the application of computers to tasks such as playing chess – with IBM's Deep Blue claiming victory, in 1997, over a series of matches with the then world champion, Gary Kasparov (see Hsu, 2002) – or simulating conversation – now a routine occurrence in a number of contexts, including automated telephony – both of which are referenced in *2001: A Space Odyssey*, and hinted at in *Alphaville*, have brought us closer to the evolutionary struggle between human and computer that Kubrick projected, even if the idea of this scenario occurring by 2001 can now, in retrospect, be seen as some way off.

Last, in terms of major shifts in the computer's fundamental characteristics, one can point to the notion of interactivity, closely linked to the aforementioned principles of real-time and graphical computing, on which interaction is typically predicated. By the end of this period, ideas concerning interactive systems and methods for generating and manipulating graphics (and, in turn, moving images), while not entirely successful in practice, and directed towards a limited notion of interactivity in terms of complexity, nevertheless signalled the potential for the interactive engagement between film-maker and computer (as a precursor to the direct involvement of the spectator, reconfigured as an active participant, in terms of a more advanced understanding of interactivity). The intuitive input of the film-maker, as programmer, was envisaged to occur through the use of displays, in conjunction with input peripherals such as the newly invented mouse (see English *et al.*, 1967), which remained experimental, in the 1970s, but which are now standard in a broader culture in which interactivity is central.

Indeed, in the dawning digital age, one can identify parallels and precursors to a plethora of contemporary developments. It is beyond the purview of this particular study to chart the full complexity of these practices, the entire spectrum of activities variously described as 'future cinema' (Shaw and Weibel, 2003), 'new digital cinema' (Willis, 2005) or 'cinema in the digital age' (Rombe, 2009), among other terms. The intention is simply to hint at some of the continuities (and discontinuities) that constitute this period's legacy, in its relation to the shifting boundaries of our contemporary screen culture, expanded beyond even Gene Youngblood's notion of 'expanded cinema' (1970; for continuing resonances, see Marchessault and Lord, 2007), which captured a *Zeitgeist* in pointing to the changing sites and practices of cinema during an earlier period of digital shift.

This study, as a historical account, necessarily suggests further developments beyond this coda or conclusion. Yet, in terms of a more sustained treatment, the proliferation of the personal computer, the emergence of the Web, the rise of video games and other key advances associated with the computer's evolution in more recent decades, collectively represent a next chapter in the history of cinema's engagement with computers, and belong in a separate work (or works). In considering the particular expressions of cinema at the dawn of the digital age, we can acknowledge what comes next, while also drawing a line at a symbolic historical cusp.

Conclusion

In the decades since the computer's initial proliferation, as functional performance has improved and as digital technology has become ever more practicable (faster, smaller, cheaper and so on), our digital screen culture has expanded exponentially. The moving images produced at the dawn of the digital age may seem a world away from contemporary discourses and expressions, yet it is in these beginnings that we can see precedents for much of the cinema of today.

It is often the artist who explores the potential of new technology, foreshadowing in their work the wider impact of technological change. 'The artist', wrote Marshall McLuhan, 'picks up the message of cultural and technological challenge decades before its transforming impact occurs. He, then, builds models or Noah's arks for facing the change that is at hand' (1964, p. 65). Notably, McLuhan's conception of the artist was much broader than usual definitions. 'The artist', he continued, 'is the man in any field, scientific or humanistic, who grasps the implications of his actions and of new knowledge in his own time. He is the man of integral awareness' (1964, p. 65).

The cinema explored in the preceding chapters can be seen as one such 'Noah's ark', with 'artists', in the sense that McLuhan intended – whether film-makers, most obviously, or the scientists and engineers who played a vital part in establishing the computer as a cinematic tool, or those whose collective imaginings propelled cultural responses and helped fuel a flourishing technological imaginary – at the forefront of developments only later taken up by the cultural mainstream. It is the hope of this study that this 'Noah's ark' will continue its journey into the future, illuminating the screen culture of today as it sails ever onward towards tomorrow.

Filmography

2001: A Space Odyssey (1968, Stanley Kubrick)

Alphaville [*Alphaville, une étrange aventure de Lemmy Caution*] (1965, Jean-Luc Godard)

Arabesque (1975, John Whitney)

Babbage (1968, Charles and Ray Eames)

Binary Bit Patterns (1969, Michael Whitney)

Byjina Flores (1964, John Whitney, Jr)

Calculated Movements (1985, Larry Cuba)

Catalog (1961, John Whitney)

Cibernetik 5.3 (1965–9, John Stehura)

Collideoscope (1966, Stan VanDerBeek)

Colossus: The Forbin Project (1970, Joseph Sargent)

A Computer Glossary (1968, Charles and Ray Eames)

Computer Landscape (1971, Charles and Ray Eames)

Computer Perspective (1972, Charles and Ray Eames)

A Computer Technique for the Production of Animated Movies (1964, Kenneth C. Knowlton)

Desk Set (1957, Walter Lang)

Dr. Strangelove or: How I Learned to Stop Worrying and Love the Bomb (1964, Stanley Kubrick)

Experiments in Motion Graphics (1967–8, John Whitney)

The Film Art of John Whitney, Sr. (1975, John Musilli, for the CBS television series *Camera Three*)

Five Abstract Film Exercises (1943–4, John and James Whitney)

Forbidden Planet (1956, Fred M. Wilcox)

Force, Mass and Motion (1965, Frank Sinden)

Futureworld (1976, Richard T. Heffron)

Gog (1954, Herbert Strock)

Homage to Rameau (1967, John Whitney)

Hummingbird (1967, Charles A. Csuri)

IBM Museum (1968, Charles and Ray Eames)

The Invisible Boy (1957, Herman Hoffman)
Lady in the Lake (1946, Robert Montgomery)
Lapis (1966, James Whitney)
Man and His World (1967, Stan VanDerBeek)
Matrix I (1971, John Whitney)
Matrix II (1972, John Whitney)
Matrix III (1972, John Whitney)
Metropolis (Fritz Lang, 1927)
Modern Times (Charles Chaplin, 1936)
Olympiad (1971, Lillian Schwartz)
On Guard! (1956, IBM Military Products Division)
Permutations (1968, John Whitney)
Pixillation (1970, Lillian Schwartz)
Poemfield #1 (1967, Stan VanDerBeek)
Poemfield #2 (1967, Stan VanDerBeek)
Poemfield #7 (1971, Stan VanDerBeek)
Portrait of a Company (1963, Albert and David Maysles)
Simulation of a Two-Gyro, Gravity-Gradient Attitude Control System (1963, Edward E. Zajac)
Stan VanDerBeek: The Computer Generation!! (1972, John Musilli, for the CBS television series *Camera Three*)
Stan VanDerBeekiana (1968, Nick Havinga, for the CBS television series *Camera Three*)
Symmetricks (1972, Stan VanDerBeek)
Terminal Self (1971, John Whitney, Jr)
Three-Dimensional Computer-Generated Movies (1965, A. Michael Noll)
Tron (1982, Steven Lisberger)
Two Space (1979, Larry Cuba)
Westworld (1973, Michael Crichton)
Yantra (1957, James Whitney)
Your Lips 1–3 (1970–1, Malcolm Le Grice)

Bibliography

Abbate, Janet (1999) *Inventing the Internet*, Cambridge, Massachusetts: MIT Press.

Agel, Jérôme (ed.) (1970) *The Making of Kubrick's* 2001, New York: New American Library.

Anon. (1952) '"Brain" Seen Used in Office Routine', *New York Times* (18 March), p. 34.

Anon. (1954) 'Electronic "Brain" Open for Business', *New York Times* (14 July), p. 13.

Anon. (1956) 'Transport News: "Brain" Is Hired', *New York Times* (23 December), section 5, p. 11.

Anon. (1957a) 'Calculatin' Emmy', *Business Machines* vol. 40 no. 7 (5 July), p. 12.

Anon. (1957b) 'IBM President Honored by Sales Executive Club', *Business Machines* vol. 40 no. 10 (27 September), pp. 3–4.

Anon. (1967a) 'A Film Revolution to Blitz Man's Mind', *Life* vol. 63 no. 2 (14 July), pp. 20–8c.

Anon. (1967b) 'Art and Science: Two Worlds Merge', *Bell Telephone Magazine* vol. 46 no. 6 (November/December), pp. 12–19.

Anon. (1968) 'The Luminous Art of the Computer', *Life* vol. 65 no. 19 (8 November), pp. 52–8.

Ascott, Roy (1964) 'The Construction of Change', *Cambridge Opinion* vol. 41 (January), pp. 37–42.

Asimov, Isaac (1940) 'Strange Playfellow', *Super Science Stories* (September), pp. 67–77. Reprinted as 'Robbie' in (1950) *I, Robot*, New York: Gnome Press.

– (1942) 'Runaround', *Astounding Science Fiction* (March), pp. 94–103.

Babbage, Charles (1832) *On the Economy of Machinery and Manufactures*, London: Charles Knight.

– (1864) *Passages from the Life of a Philosopher*, London: Longman, Green, Longman, Roberts, and Green.

Ballard, J. G. (1975) 'Some Words about *Crash!*', *Foundation* vol. 9 (November), pp. 45–54. Originally published, translated into French, in the first French edition of Ballard's novel (1974) *Crash!*, Paris: Calmann-Lévy.

Baran, Paul (1964) 'On Distributed Communications Networks', *IEEE Transactions on Communications* CS-12 no. 1 (March), pp. 1–9.

Bashe, Charles J. (1982) 'The SSEC in Historical Perspective', *Annals of the History of Computing* vol. 4 no. 4 (October), pp. 296–312.

Bashe, Charles J. *et al.* (1985) *IBM's Early Computers*, Cambridge, Massachusetts: MIT Press.

Bataille, Maurice (1971) 'The Gamma 60: The Computer That Was Ahead of Its Time', *Honeywell Computer Journal* vol. 5 no. 3, pp. 99–105.

Bijker, Wiebe E. (1995) *Of Bicycles, Bakelites, and Bulbs: Toward a Theory of Sociotechnical Change*, Cambridge, Massachusetts: MIT Press.

Bolter, Jay David and Grusin, Richard (1999) *Remediation: Understanding New Media*, Cambridge, Massachusetts: MIT Press.

Bordwell, David, Staiger, Janet and Thompson, Kristin (1985) *The Classical Hollywood Cinema: Film Style and Mode of Production to 1960*, New York: Columbia University Press.

Bordwell, David and Staiger, Janet (1985) 'Technology, Style and Mode of Production' in David Bordwell, Janet Staiger and Kristin Thompson, *The Classical Hollywood Cinema: Film Style and Mode of Production to 1960*, New York: Columbia University Press, pp. 243–61.

Bordwell, David and Thompson, Kristin (1993) 'Technological Change and Classical Film Style' in Tino Balio, *Grand Design: Hollywood as a Modern Business Enterprise, 1930–1939*, New York: Charles Scribner's Sons, pp. 109–41. This text is a revision of Bordwell, David and Staiger, Janet (1985) 'Technology, Style and Mode of Production' in David Bordwell, Janet Staiger and Kristin Thompson, *The Classical Hollywood Cinema: Film Style and Mode of Production to 1960*, New York: Columbia University Press, pp. 243–61.

Boyd, David (1978) 'Mode and Meaning in *2001*', *Journal of Popular Film* no. 6 (September), pp. 202–15.

Brand, Stewart (1972) '*Spacewar*: Fanatic Life and Symbolic Death among the Computer Bums', *Rolling Stone* (7 December), pp. 33–8.

Branigan, Edward R. (1984) *Point of View in the Cinema: A Theory of Narration and Subjectivity in Classical Film*, New York: Mouton.

Braverman, Harry (1974) *Labor and Monopoly Capital: The Degradation of Work in the Twentieth Century*, New York: Monthly Review Press.

Burch, Noël (1990) *Life to Those Shadows*, translated from the French by Ben Brewster, London: BFI.

Burroughs, Edgar Rice (1914) *Tarzan of the Apes*, Chicago, Illinois: A. C. McClurg.

Bush, Vannevar (1945) 'As We May Think', *Atlantic Monthly* vol. 176 no. 1 (July), pp. 101–8.

Campbell-Kelly, Martin and Aspray, William (2004, second edition) *Computer: A History of the Information Machine*, Boulder, Colorado: Westview Press.

Ceruzzi, Paul E. (2003, second edition) *A History of Modern Computing*, Cambridge, Massachusetts: MIT Press.

Chion, Michel (2001) *Kubrick's Cinema Odyssey*, translated from the French by Claudia Gorbman, London: BFI.

Citron, Jack and Whitney, John (1968) 'CAMP – Computer Assisted Movie Production', *AFIPS Conference Proceedings* vol. 33 no. 2, pp. 1299–305.

Clarke, Arthur C. (1958) *Voice across the Sea*, New York: Harper and Brothers.

– (1968) *2001: A Space Odyssey*, New York: New American Library.

– (1972) *The Lost Worlds of* 2001, London: Sidgwick and Jackson.

Claus, Jürgen (2003) 'Stan VanDerBeek: An Early Space Art Pioneer', *Leonardo* vol. 36 no. 3 (June), p. 229.

Colatrella, Carol (2001) 'From *Desk Set* to *The Net*: Women and Computing Technology in Hollywood Films', *Canadian Review of American Studies* vol. 31 no. 2, pp. 1–14.

Cournot, Michel (1965) 'Les robots sont là!', *Le Nouvel Observateur* (in French) (6 May), pp. 2–3.

Crichton, Michael (1974) *Westworld*, New York: Bantam Books.

Csuri, Charles A. (ed.) (1970) *Interactive Sound and Visual Systems*, Columbus: Ohio State University Press.

Csuri, Charles A. and Shaffer, James (1968) 'Art, Computers and Mathematics', *AFIPS Conference Proceedings* vol. 33 no. 2, pp. 1293–8.

Darke, Chris (2005) *Alphaville*, London: I. B. Tauris.

Davis, Douglas M. (1968) 'Art and Technology – The New Combine', *Art in America* vol. 56 no. 1 (January–February), pp. 28–37.

– (1973) *Art and the Future: A History/Prophecy of the Collaboration between Science, Technology and Art*, New York: Praeger.

Demos, Gary (2005) 'My Personal History in the Early Explorations of Computer Graphics', *Visual Computer* vol. 21 no. 12 (December), pp. 961–78.

Ellul, Jacques (1964) *The Technological Society*, translated from the French by John Wilkinson, New York: Alfred A. Knopf (originally published in French in 1954).

Elsaesser, Thomas (2004) 'The New Film History as Media Archaeology', *Cinémas: revue d'études cinématographiques* vol. 14 nos 2–3, pp. 75–117.

– (2006) 'Early Film History and Multi-Media: An Archaeology of Possible Futures?' in Wendy Hui Kyong Chun and Thomas Keenan (eds) *New Media, Old Media: A History and Theory Reader*, London: Routledge, pp. 13–25.

Elsaesser, Thomas and Hoffmann, Kay (eds) (1998) *Cinema Futures: Cain, Abel or Cable? The Screen Arts in the Digital Age*, Amsterdam: Amsterdam University Press.

Éluard, Paul (1926) *Capitale de la douleur* (in French), Paris: Gallimard.

– (1946) *Le dur désir de durer* (in French), Paris: Arnold-Bordas.

– (1951) *Le phénix* (in French), Paris: GLM.

English, William K., Engelbart, Douglas C. and Berman, Melyvn L. (1967) 'Display-Selection Techniques for Text Manipulation', *IEEE Transactions on Human Factors in Electronics* HFE-8 no. 1 (March), pp. 5–15.

Fetter, William A. (1965) *Computer Graphics in Communication*, New York: McGraw-Hill.

Franke, Herbert W. (1971) *Computer Graphics, Computer Art*, translated from the German by Gustav Metzger, London: Phaidon Press.

Frewin, Anthony (ed.) (2005) *Are We Alone? The Stanley Kubrick Extraterrestrial-Intelligence Interviews*, London: Elliott and Thompson.

Fuller, R. Buckminster (1954) US Pat. 2682235. *Geodesic Dome Building Construction.* Granted on 29 June, originally filed on 12 December 1951.

– (1969a) *Operating Manual for Spaceship Earth*, Carbondale: Southern Illinois University Press.

– (1969b) *Utopia or Oblivion: The Prospects for Humanity*, New York: Overlook Press.

Gibson, William (1984) *Neuromancer*, London: Gollancz.

Godard, Jean-Luc (1966) *Alphaville: Screenplay*, translated from the French by Peter Whitehead, London: Lorrimer Films.

Gomery, Douglas (1985a) 'Technological Film History' in Robert C. Allen and Douglas Gomery, *Film History: Theory and Practice*, New York: Alfred A. Knopf, pp. 109–30.

– (1985b) 'The Coming of Sound: Technological Change in the American Film Industry' in Tino Balio (ed.) *The American Film Industry* (revised edition), Madison: University of Wisconsin Press, pp. 229–51. This text is a revision of (1976) 'The Coming of the Talkies: Invention, Innovation, and Diffusion' in Tino Balio (ed.) *The American Film Industry*, Madison: University of Wisconsin Press, pp. 193–211.

– (2005) *The Coming of Sound*, London: Routledge.

Grundmann, Roy (2004) 'Masters of Ceremony: Media Demonstration as Performance in Three Instances of Expanded Cinema', *Velvet Light Trap* vol. 54 (Fall), pp. 48–64.

Gunning, Tom (1986) 'The Cinema of Attraction: Early Film, Its Spectator and the Avant-Garde', *Wide Angle* vol. 8 nos 3–4, pp. 63–70.

– (1989) '"Primitive" Cinema – A Frame-up? or The Trick's on Us', *Cinema Journal* vol. 28 no. 2 (Winter), pp. 3–12.

Hacker, Barton C. and Grimwood, James M. (1977) *On the Shoulders of Titans: A History of Project Gemini*, Washington, DC: Scientific and Technical Information Office, National Aeronautics and Space Administration.

Hall, Eldon C. (1996) *Journey to the Moon: The History of the Apollo Guidance Computer*, Reston, Virginia: American Institute of Aeronautics and Astronautics.

Higgins, Dick (1966) 'Intermedia', *Something Else Newsletter* vol. 1 no. 1 (February), unpaginated.

Hsu, Feng-hsiung (2002) *Behind Deep Blue: Building the Computer That Defeated the World Chess Champion*, Princeton, New Jersey: Princeton University Press.

Kahn, Herman (1960) *On Thermonuclear War*, Princeton, New Jersey: Princeton University Press.

Kennedy, John F. (1962) *Public Papers of the Presidents of the United States, John F. Kennedy, 1961*, Washington, DC: United States Government Printing Office.

King, Augusta Ada (Countess of Lovelace) (credited in this instance as 'A. L. L.') (1843) translator's notes throughout and following Luigi Federico Menabrea's 'Sketch of the Analytical Engine Invented by Charles Babbage Esq.' in Richard Taylor (ed.) *Scientific Memoirs, Selected from The Transactions of Foreign Academies of Science and Learned Societies and from Foreign Journals, Vol. 3*, London: Richard and John E. Taylor, pp. 666–731.

Klüver, Billy (ed.) (1966) *Nine Evenings: Theatre and Engineering*, New York: Foundation for the Performing Arts.

Klüver, Billy and Rauschenberg, Robert (1967) *EAT News* vol. 1 no. 2 (1 June).

Knowlton, Kenneth C. (1964) 'A Computer Technique for Producing Animated Movies', *AFIPS Conference Proceedings* vol. 25, pp. 67–87.

– (1965) 'Computer-Produced Movies', *Science* vol. 150 no. 3700 (26 November), pp. 1116–20.

– (1966) 'Computer-Generated Movies, Designs and Diagrams', *Design Quarterly* vols 66/67, pp. 58–63.

– (1968) 'Computer-Animated Movies' in Jasia Reichardt (ed.) *Cybernetic Serendipity: The Computer and the Arts*, London: Studio International, pp. 67–8.

– (1970) 'Computer Films', *Filmmakers Newsletter* vol. 4 no. 2 (December), pp. 14–23.

– (1972) 'Collaborations with Artists – A Programmer's Reflections' in Frieder Nake and Azriel Rosenfeld (eds) *Graphic Languages: Proceedings of the IFIP Working Conference on Graphic Languages*, Amsterdam: North-Holland Publishing, pp. 399–418.

– (1976) 'Ken Knowlton' in Ruth Leavitt (ed.) *Artist and Computer*, New York: Harmony Books, pp. 65–9.

– (2001) 'On Frustrations of Collaborating with Artists', *Computer Graphics* vol. 35 no. 3 (August), pp. 22–4.

– (2005a) 'Portrait of the Artist as a Young Scientist', *YLEM Journal* vol. 25 no. 2 (January/February), pp. 8–11.

– (2005b) author correspondence, 11 March.

– (2006) author correspondence, 26 July.

Kranz, Stewart (1974) 'Stan VanDerBeek: Multimedia Artist, Stony Point, New York' in *Science and Technology in the Arts: A Tour through the Realm of Science/Art*, New York: Van Nostrand Reinhold Company, pp. 237–42.

Latour, Bruno (1987) *Science in Action: How to Follow Scientists and Engineers through Society*, Cambridge, Massachusetts: Harvard University Press.

Le Grice, Malcolm (1974) 'Computer Film as Film Art' in John Halas (ed.) *Computer Animation*, London: Focal Press, pp. 161–8.

– (2001) *Experimental Cinema in the Digital Age*, London: BFI.

Levinson, Paul (1999) *Digital McLuhan: A Guide to the Information Millennium*, London: Routledge.

Lewis, J. A. and Zajac, Edward E. (1964) 'A Two-Gyro, Gravity-Gradient Satellite Attitude Control System', *Bell System Technical Journal* vol. 43 no. 6 (November), pp. 2705–65.

Licklider, J. C. R. (1960) 'Man–Computer Symbiosis', *IRE Transactions on Human Factors in Electronics* HFE-1 (March), pp. 4–11.

– (1968) 'Computer Graphics as a Medium of Artistic Expression' in Metropolitan Museum of Art (ed.) *Computers and Their Potential Applications in Museums*, New York: Arno Press, pp. 273–301.

Lieberman, Henry R. (1967) 'Art and Science Proclaim Alliance in Avant-Garde Loft', *New York Times* (11 October), p. 49.

Malone, Cheryl K. (2002) 'Imagining Information Retrieval in the Library: *Desk Set* in Historical Context', *IEEE Annals of the History of Computing* vol. 24 no. 3 (July–September), pp. 14–22.

Mancia, Adrienne and Van Dyke, Willard (1967) 'Four Artists as Film-Makers', *Art in America* vol. 55 no. 1 (January–February), pp. 64–73.

Maney, Kevin (2003) *The Maverick and His Machine: Thomas Watson, Sr. and the Making of IBM*, Hoboken, New Jersey: John Wiley.

Manovich, Lev (2001) *The Language of New Media*, Cambridge, Massachusetts: MIT Press.

Marchessault, Janine (2007) 'Multi-Screens and Future Cinema: The Labyrinth Project at Expo 67' in Janine Marchessault and Susan Lord (eds) *Fluid Screens, Expanded Cinema*, Toronto: University of Toronto Press, pp. 29–51.

Marchessault, Janine and Lord, Susan (eds) (2007) *Fluid Screens, Expanded Cinema*, Toronto: University of Toronto Press.

Marcuse, Herbert (1964) *One-Dimensional Man: Studies in the Ideology of Advanced Industrial Society*, Boston, Massachusetts: Beacon Press.

– (1969) *An Essay on Liberation*, Boston, Massachusetts: Beacon Press.

Marinetti, Filippo Tommaso *et al.* (1972) 'The Futurist Cinema' in Richard W. Flint (ed.) *Marinetti: Selected Writings*, translated from the Italian by Richard W. Flint and Arthur A.

Coppotelli, New York: Farrar, Straus & Giroux (originally published in Italian in 1916), pp. 130–4.

Martin, Adrian (2004) 'Recital: Three Lyrical Interludes in Godard' in Michael Temple, James S. Williams and Michael Witt (eds) *For Ever Godard*, London: Black Dog Publishing, pp. 252–71.

Marx, Karl (1887) *Capital (Volume 1: The Process of Production of Capital)*, translated from the German (from the third, revised edition, 1883), by Samuel Moore and Edward Aveling, London: Swan Sonnenschein, Lowrey (originally published in German in 1867).

Matheson, T. J. (1992) 'Marcuse, Ellul, and the Science-Fiction Film: Negative Responses to Technology', *Science-Fiction Studies* vol. 19 no. 3, pp. 326–39.

McCartney, Scott (1999) *ENIAC: The Triumphs and Tragedies of the World's First Computer*, New York: Walker.

McClean, Shilo T. (2007) *Digital Storytelling: The Narrative Power of Visual Effects in Film*, Cambridge, Massachusetts: MIT Press.

McHale, John (1969) *The Future of the Future*, New York: George Braziller.

McLuhan, Marshall (1964) *Understanding Media: The Extensions of Man*, New York: McGraw-Hill.

McLuhan, Marshall and Fiore, Quentin (1967) *The Medium Is the Massage: An Inventory of Effects*, New York: Bantam Books.

– (1968) *War and Peace in the Global Village*, New York: McGraw-Hill.

Midbon, Mark (1990) 'Creation Machines: Stanley Kubrick's View of Computers in *2001*', *Computers and Society* vol. 20 no. 4 (December), pp. 7–12.

Minsky, Marvin L. (1979) 'Computer Science and the Representation of Knowledge' in Michael L. Dertouzos and Joel Moses (eds) *The Computer Age: A Twenty-Year View*, Cambridge, Massachusetts: MIT Press, pp. 392–421.

– (2006a) author correspondence, 31 October.

– (2006b) author correspondence, 3 November.

Moore, Gordon E. (1965) 'Cramming More Components onto Integrated Circuits', *Electronics Magazine* vol. 38 no. 8 (19 April), pp. 114–17.

Moritz, William (1997) 'Digital Harmony: The Life of John Whitney, Computer Animation Pioneer', *Animation World Magazine* vol. 2 no. 5 (August), pp. 29–31.

Mumford, Lewis (1934) *Technics and Civilization*, New York: Harcourt, Brace.

– (1967) *The Myth of the Machine, Vol. 1: Technics and Human Development*, New York: Harcourt, Brace, Jovanovich.

– (1970) *The Myth of the Machine, Vol. 2: The Pentagon of Power*, New York: Harcourt, Brace, Jovanovich.

Neale, Steve (1985) *Cinema and Technology: Image, Sound, Colour*, London: BFI and Macmillan Education.

Nelson, Theodor H. (1974) *Computer Lib/Dream Machines*, Chicago, Illinois: self-published.

Newell, Allen, Simon, Herbert A. and Shaw, J. Cliff (1958) 'Chess-playing Programs and the Problem of Complexity', *IBM Journal of Research and Development* vol. 2 (October), pp. 320–35.

Noll, A. Michael (1965a) 'Stereographic Projections by Digital Computer', *Computers and Automation* vol. 14 no. 5 (May), pp. 32–4.

– (1965b) 'Computer-generated Three-Dimensional Movies', *Computers and Automation* vol. 14 no. 11 (November), pp. 20–3.

– (1967a) 'Computers and the Visual Arts' in Martin Krampen and Peter Seitz (eds) *Design and Planning 2: Computers in Design and Communication*, New York: Hastings House, pp. 64–79. This text is a revision of (1966) 'Computers and the Visual Arts', *Design Quarterly* vols 66/67, pp. 64–71.

– (1967b) 'A Computer Technique for Displaying *n*-Dimensional Hyperobjects', *Communications of the ACM* vol. 10 no. 8 (August), pp. 469–73.

– (1967c) 'The Digital Computer as a Creative Medium', *IEEE Spectrum* vol. 4 no. 10 (October), pp. 89–95.

– (1968) 'Computer Animation and the Fourth Dimension', *AFIPS Conference Proceedings* vol. 33 no. 2, pp. 1279–83. Reworked as (1971) 'Animation in a Four Dimensional Space', *Filmmakers Newsletter* vol. 4 no. 5 (March), pp. 29–32.

– (1994) 'The Beginnings of Computer Art in the United States: A Memoir', *Leonardo* vol. 27 no. 1, pp. 39–44.

– (2006) author correspondence, 2 November.

Ordway, Frederick I. (1970a) 'The Missing Links?' in Jérôme Agel (ed.) *The Making of Kubrick's* 2001, New York: New American Library, pp. 193–8.

– (1970b) '*2001: A Space Odyssey*', *Spaceflight* vol. 12 no. 3 (March), pp. 110–17.

Paik, Nam June (1966) 'Cybernated Art' in Ay-O *et al.*, *Manifestos*, New York: Something Else Press (A Great Bear Pamphlet), p. 24.

Paik, Nam June and Hanhardt, John G. (2000) *The Worlds of Nam June Paik*, New York: Solomon R. Guggenheim Foundation.

Patterson, Zabet (2009) 'From the Gun Controller to the Mandala: The Cybernetic Cinema of John and James Whitney', *Grey Room* vol. 36 (Summer), pp. 36–57.

Pierson, Michele (2002) *Special Effects: Still in Search of Wonder*, New York: Columbia University Press.

Prehoda, Robert (1968) '*2001: A Space Odyssey*', *The Futurist* vol. 2 no. 3 (June), pp. 52–3.

Pugh, Emerson W. (1995) *Building IBM: Shaping an Industry and Its Technology*, Cambridge, Massachusetts: MIT Press.

Raphael, Bertram (1976) *The Thinking Computer: Mind inside Matter*, San Francisco, California: W. H. Freeman.

Redmond, Kent C. and Smith, Thomas M. (2000) *From Whirlwind to MITRE: The R&D Story of the SAGE Air Defense Computer*, Cambridge, Massachusetts: MIT Press.

Reichardt, Jasia (ed.) (1968) *Cybernetic Serendipity: The Computer and the Arts*, London: Studio International.

– (1971) *The Computer in Art*, London: Studio Vista.

Renan, Sheldon (1967) *An Introduction to the American Underground Film*, New York: E. P. Dutton.

Robinson, David (1966) 'Two for the Sci-fi', *Sight and Sound* vol. 35 no. 2 (Spring), pp. 57–61.

Rodowick, D. N. (2007) *The Virtual Life of Film*, Cambridge, Massachusetts: Harvard University Press.

Rombe, Nicholas (2009) *Cinema in the Digital Age*, London: Wallflower Press.

Rosenthal, Raymond (ed.) (1968) *McLuhan: Pro and Con*, New York: Funk and Wagnalls.

Ross, Kristin (1995) *Fast Cars, Clean Bodies: Decolonization and the Reordering of French Culture*, Cambridge, Massachusetts: MIT Press.

Schrage, Michael (1982) 'Computer Animation Comes of Age in a Studio on "Dopey Drive"', *Smithsonian* vol. 13 (July), pp. 86–95.

Schwartz, Lillian F. (1974) 'The Artist and Computer Animation' in John Halas (ed.) *Computer Animation*, New York: Hastings House, pp. 159–60.

– (1976) 'Lillian Schwartz' in Ruth Leavitt (ed.) *Artist and Computer*, New York: Harmony Books, pp. 107–8.

Schwartz, Lillian F. with Schwartz, Laurens R. (1992) *The Computer Artist's Handbook: Concepts, Techniques, and Applications*, New York: W. W. Norton.

Shannon, Claude E. (1950) 'Programming a Computer for Playing Chess', *Philosophical Magazine* (Series 7) vol. 41 no. 314 (March), pp. 256–75.

Shaw, Jeffrey and Weibel, Peter (eds) (2003) *Future Cinema: The Cinematic Imaginary after Film*, Cambridge, Massachusetts: MIT Press.

Shelley, Mary W. (1818) *Frankenstein; or, the Modern Prometheus*, London: Lackington, Hughes, Harding, Mavor, and Jones.

Silverman, Kaja and Farocki, Harun (1998) *Speaking about Godard*, New York: New York University Press.

Simon, Herbert A. and Newell, Allen (1958) 'Heuristic Problem Solving: The Next Advance in Operations Research', *Operations Research* vol. 6 no. 1 (January–February), pp. 1–10.

Sinden, Frank W. (1965) 'Synthetic Cinematography', *Perspective* vol. 7 no. 4, pp. 279–89.

– (1967) 'Principles and Programming of Animation' in Martin Krampen and Peter Seitz (eds) *Design and Planning 2: Computers in Design and Communication*, New York: Hastings House, pp. 80–5.

Springer, Claudia (1991) 'The Pleasure of the Interface', *Screen* vol. 32 no. 3 (Autumn), pp. 303–23.

Stork, David G. (1997) 'Scientist on the Set: An Interview with Marvin Minsky' in (ed.) *Hal's Legacy: 2001's Computer as Dream and Reality*, Cambridge, Massachusetts: MIT Press, pp. 15–31.

Stringham, W. Irving (1880) 'Regular Figures in *n*-Dimensional Space', *American Journal of Mathematics* vol. 3 no. 1 (March), pp. 1–14.

Sutherland, Ivan E. (1963) 'Sketchpad: A Man–Machine Graphical Communication System', *AFIPS Conference Proceedings* vol. 23, pp. 329–46.

Sutton, Gloria (2003) 'Stan VanDerBeek's Movie-Drome: Networking the Subject' in Jeffrey Shaw and Peter Weibel (eds) *Future Cinema: The Cinematic Imaginary after Film*, Cambridge, Massachusetts: MIT Press, pp. 136–43.

Taylor, Frederick Winslow (1911) *The Principles of Scientific Management*, New York: Harper and Brothers.

Telotte, J. P. (1995) *Replications: A Robotic History of the Science Fiction Film*, Urbana: University of Illinois Press. The chapter on *Westworld* is a revision of (1992) '*Westworld, Futureworld*, and the World's Obscenity' in Nicholas Ruddick (ed.) *State of the Fantastic: Studies in the Theory and Practice of Fantastic Literature and Film*, Westport, Connecticut: Greenwood Press, pp. 179–88.

Toffler, Alvin (1970) *Future Shock*, New York: Random House.

Tozzi, Romano V. (1957) '*Desk Set*', *Films in Review* vol. 8 no. 6 (June–July), pp. 279–80.

Trumbull, Douglas (1968) 'Creating Special Effects for *2001: A Space Odyssey*', *American Cinematographer* vol. 49 no. 6 (June), pp. 416–19, 451–5.

Tuchman, Maurice (ed.) (1971) *A Report on the Art and Technology Program of the Los Angeles County Museum of Art, 1967–1971*, Los Angeles, California: Los Angeles County Museum of Art.

Turing, Alan M. (1936) 'On Computable Numbers, with an Application to the *Entscheidungsproblem*', *Proceedings of the London Mathematical Society* (Series 2) no. 42, pp. 230–65.

– (1950) 'Computing Machinery and Intelligence', *Mind* vol. 59 no. 236 (October), pp. 433–60.

VanDerBeek, Stan (1966) '"Culture:Intercom" and Expanded Cinema: A Proposal and Manifesto', *Film Culture* vol. 40 (Spring), pp. 15–18.

– (1970) 'New Talent – The Computer', *Art in America* vol. 58 no. 1 (January–February), pp. 86–91.

– (1971) 'Media W/rap-Around or A Man with No Close', *Filmmakers Newsletter* vol. 4 no. 5 (March), pp. 20–5.

Von Neumann, John (1945) *First Draft of a Report on the EDVAC*, Philadelphia: Moore School of Electrical Engineering, University of Pennsylvania.

Warrick, Patricia S. (1980) *The Cybernetic Imagination in Science Fiction*, Cambridge, Massachusetts: MIT Press.

Weizenbaum, Joseph (1966) 'ELIZA – A Computer Program for the Study of Natural Language Communication between Man and Machine', *Communications of the ACM* vol. 9 no. 1 (January), pp. 36–45.

– (1976) *Computer Power and Human Reason: From Judgment to Calculation*, San Francisco, California: W. H. Freeman.

White, Jr, Lynn (1962) *Medieval Technology and Social Change*, Oxford: Clarendon Press.

Whitney, John (1965) 'ASID: Talk-Design Conference, Catalina, 1962', *Film Culture* vol. 37 (Summer), pp. 21 4.

– (1968) '*Permutations*' in Jasia Reichardt (ed.) *Cybernetic Serendipity: The Computer and the Arts*, London: Studio International, pp. 65–6.

– (1970a) 'An Interview with John Whitney', *Film Comment* vol. 6 no. 3 (Fall), pp. 28–33.

– (1970b) 'John Whitney 2', *Film Comment* vol. 6 no. 3 (Fall), pp. 34–8.

– (1971a) 'Animation Mechanisms', *American Cinematographer* vol. 52 no. 1 (January), pp. 26–31.

– (1971b) 'A Computer Art for the Video Picture Wall', *Art International* vol. 15 no. 7 (20 September), pp. 35–6.

– (1972a) 'John Whitney Interview, Conducted by Richard Brick, 12/30/1969', *Film Culture* vols 53–54–55 (Spring), pp. 39–73.

– (1972b) 'Excerpts of Talk Given at California Institute of Technology – 3/21/1968', *Film Culture* vols 53–54–55 (Spring), pp. 73–8.

– (1972c) 'Notes on *Matrix*', *Film Culture* vols 53–54–55 (Spring), pp. 79–80.

– (1976) 'Computational Periodics' in Ruth Leavitt (ed.) *Artist and Computer*, New York: Harmony Books, pp. 80–1.

– (1980) *Digital Harmony: On the Complementarity of Music and Visual Art*, Peterborough, New Hampshire: Byte Books.

– (1981) 'Motion Control: An Overview', *American Cinematographer* vol. 62 no. 12 (December), pp. 1220–3, 1236–7, 1242–3, 1261–3.

Whitney, Jr, John (1973) 'Creating the Special Effects for *Westworld*', *American Cinematographer* vol. 54 no. 11 (November), pp. 1477–80.

– (2007) author correspondence, 16 January.

Whitney, Michael (1997) 'The Whitney Archive: A Fulfillment of a Dream', *Animation World Magazine* vol. 2 no. 5 (August), pp. 57–8.

Wiener, Norbert (1948) *Cybernetics, or Control and Communication in the Animal and the Machine*, Cambridge, Massachusetts: Technology Press.

– (1950) *The Human Use of Human Beings: Cybernetics and Society*, Boston, Massachusetts: Houghton Mifflin.

Willis, Holly (2005) *New Digital Cinema: Reinventing the Moving Image*, London: Wallflower Press.

Winston, Brian (1996) *Technologies of Seeing: Photography, Cinematography and Television*, London: BFI.

– (1998) *Media Technology and Society: A History: From the Telegraph to the Internet*, London: Routledge. This text is a revision of (1986) *Misunderstanding Media*, Cambridge, Massachusetts: Harvard University Press.

Youngblood, Gene (1970) *Expanded Cinema*, New York: E. P. Dutton.

Zajac, Edward E. (1964) 'Computer-made Perspective Movies as a Scientific and Communication Tool', *Communications of the ACM* vol. 7 no. 3 (March), pp. 169–70.

– (1965) 'Computer Animation: A New Scientific and Educational Tool', *Journal of the SMPTE* vol. 74 no. 11, pp. 1006–8.

– (1966) 'Film Animation by Computer', *New Scientist* vol. 29 no. 482 (10 February), pp. 346–9.

– (1967) 'Motion Picture Animation' in Fred Gruenberger (ed.) *Computer Graphics: Utility/Production/Art*, Washington, DC: Thompson Book Company, pp. 199–208.

– (2005) author correspondence, 21 November.

Zielinski, Siegfried (1999) *Audiovisions: Cinema and Television as Entr'actes in History*, translated from the German by Gloria Custance, Amsterdam: Amsterdam University Press (originally published in German in 1989).

– (2006) *Deep Time of the Media: Toward an Archaeology of Hearing and Seeing by Technical Means*, translated from the German by Gloria Custance, Cambridge, Massachusetts: MIT Press (originally published in German in 2002).

Zipser, Alfred R. (1957) 'Big Business Done in Big Computers', *New York Times* (10 February), section 3, pp. 1–2.

Index

List of Illustrations

While considerable effort has been made to correctly identify the copyright holders, this has not been possible in all cases. We apologise for any apparent negligence and any omissions or corrections brought to our attention will be remedied in any future editions.

Forbidden Planet, © Loew's Incorporated; *Invisible Boy*, Loew's Incorporated/Pan Productions/Metro-Goldwyn-Mayer; *Desk Set*, © Twentieth Century-Fox Film Corporation; *Catalog*, John Whitney; *Lapis*, James Whitney; *Yantra*, Uroboros Films; *Simulation of a Two-Gyro, Gravity-Gradient Attitude Control System*, Edward Zajac; *Metropolis*, Ufa; *Modern Times*, Charles Chaplin Corporation; *Alphaville*, Chaumiane Productions/Filmstudio; *Collideoscope*, Stan Vanderbeek Productions; *Poemfield #2*, Stan Vanderbeek Productions; *Permutations*, IBM/John Whitney; *Experiments in Motion Graphics*, John Whitney; *Colossus: The Forbin Project*, Universal Pictures; *Dr. Strangelove, Or: How I Learned to Stop Worrying and Love the Bomb*, © Hawk Films; *2001: A Space Odyssey*, © Metro-Goldwyn-Mayer; *Symmetricks*, Stan VanDerBeek; *Matrix I*, John Whitney; *Matrix II*, John Whitney; *Matrix III*, John Whitney; *Westworld*, Metro-Goldwyn-Mayer; *Terminal Self*, John Whitney, Jr; *Lady in the Lake*, © Loew's Incorporated; *Tron*, © Walt Disney Productions; *Arabesque*, John Whitney; *Two Space*, Larry Cuba.